Foxglove's
FIELD OF VIEW

Foxglove's
FIELD OF VIEW

Kingswood Press

Dedicated to all those who made it possible.
You know who you are.

First published in the UK in 2008 by Kingswood Press, Kingswood Associates, Fen Farm Cottage,
Fen Lane, New Bolingbroke, Boston, Lincolnshire PE22 7JQ

British Library Cataloguing-in-Publication Data
A catalogue record for this book
is available from the British Library

ISBN 978 0 9558139 0 0

Photographs kindly provided by PAB Photography in association with Kingswood Press.

Printed in China

CONTENTS

INTRODUCTION

In the early part of the 21st century, the countryside as we know it stands at a crossroads. Coming over the hill towards it is a storm of change greater even than the Agricultural Revolution, or the Depression of the 1930s. Rural areas are under threat from vast numbers of people with a different view of the countryside and different requirements of it, often, sadly, with no understanding of its ways and values, and what lies behind these. The pressure is on: rural people, the landscape in which they live and work, their skills and distinct way of life, are all at risk. Can the countryside survive? I believe it can, but only if we make it happen. We must speak out and educate those who have not had the good fortune to learn country ways and skills. We must not allow old values to be lost. We must share the secrets, too.

This book does just that, and deserves to be read by all those who want to learn and understand more. It tells, quietly and from profound experience, the how and why of managing the countryside, treading softly over the ground in the way of a true countryman. It shows how hunting and conservation are a part of the same great landscape, tightly woven into the everyday lives of rural people, and vital to the maintenance of the countryside we love.

If we fail this heritage, then our children and their children will grow up with a layer of concrete between themselves and the earth, never knowing or understanding the ways of the wild things or the smell of the changing seasons. That would be a loss indeed.

Ann Mallalieu

HISTORY

The Labour party threat to hunting and therefore countryside management was met with considerable opposition, starting with the Hyde Park Rally and continuing with major well-organised protests countrywide. These protests were law-abiding, but there was no mistaking the seriousness of the message: Listen to Us. Foxglove attended all the major protests and many of the smaller ones, culminating in the last great London march "Liberty and Livelihood" which had an official count of nearly 500,000 marchers and a vast number, probably equal to that, who were prevented from joining by the authorities. This was the biggest peacetime march ever seen in the UK at the time.

This is Foxglove's account of the first March, which was preceded by beacons being lit all over the country, in the British tradition.

The First London March for the Countryside 1998

We hadn't come easily, any of us. It was not just a matter of getting out of bed and going off, but of getting up hours before dawn to set livestock to rights first, of arranging other people to come in and look after our animals while we were away, or, in the case of the Scottish and Welsh groups, struggling through snow to leave their homes late on Saturday afternoon to march through London on Sunday. For every family that made the journey, there were people left behind who would dearly have liked to have come, but animals have to be tended around the clock. Every one of us in London on the first of March was casting anxious thoughts back to the livestock at home. But we had to be there.

We didn't come easily, but we came. People came in wheelchairs, on crutches, leaning heavily on sticks, in some cases having left hospital beds a little too early. From France and America they came, tiny babies came, octogenarians came, a sea of tweed and olive drab, well-worn boots, and anger. At Horsham station, the platform was swamped with more than four hundred country lovers, and the picture was repeated at railway stations all over the country, while thousands of marchers travelled in by coach. The London underground was swamped by us, trains being unable to disembark their passengers because of the congestion on the platforms. For people used to open spaces and fresh air, it was a nightmare experience, but we had to be there.

Waiting on the Embankment for the march to start, we watched coachload after coachload of passengers unload, crowding the bridge, joining behind us. Ahead the column stretched unbroken out of sight. For six hours that column marched.

We marched with brisk country strides, smiling at bemused police, returning friendly waves from those who greeted us from their windows, delighting in the banners of support hanging from the shops in St. James' Street. We marched as a true example of classless society, almost every trade and title represented, a determined army of 284,500 people, every one of whom would have been able to talk on level terms with every other one. This was not a march of country versus town, for many town people marched with us. There is many a town dweller with the countryside in his or her heart, just as many people live geographically in the country but with their souls in the town. If it is born in you to love the woods and fields and the creatures that dwell therein, if it is right for you to hunt, shoot, fish, enjoy the clean air and beautiful views, then it matters not where or how you are bred, for you are one of us. You are so very welcome here, as long as you understand and respect what makes our land the lovely place that it is, and what makes our place in it.

If you don't like cow muck on the roads, cockerels crowing, flies on dungheaps, if the ringing echo of hounds, horn and huntsman's voice calls no answering echo in your heart, we would not compel you to endure them. But we will not have outsiders' views forced upon us. We will have British food, and we will have it just the way we like it. We will hunt, shoot and fish, protect the countryside environment to allow wildlife and farming interests to flourish in tandem, and we will not be bullied.

Sitting by the Serpentine at the end of the march, watching the broad columns of country lovers pass steadily, we knew that it was a job that had to be done. We did it and went home, once again to tend our animals, in the rolling timelessness that is country life, daytime, nighttime, any season, any weather.

But when we lit our beacons last Thursday, in that most British of gestures, the flames were a symbol of the flames in our hearts. 'Sussex wunt be druv'* – and neither will any of us.

We are a huge, controlled and motivated army, and we really mean it.

Listen to us!

*This is a traditional saying about Sussex people, meaning that they will not be driven i.e. forced to do anything.

SPRING

I defy anyone to watch a field full of young lambs playing and not have an indulgent smile on their face. The little ones tear round in packs, leaping and bounding, now playing king-of-the-castle on a tree-stump, now billy-goat-gruff (you shall not pass) between the fence posts. Woolly legs are marshalled briefly under control and then hurl the tiny wavemarked bodies upwards, forwards, any way at all, and there doesn't have to be a reason. Here and there, one sleeps alone, with that tightly-shut slumber of the very young, a little piece of rag upon the green. Ewes doze or cud or rise heavily and reluctantly to let their own little collection of pipe-cleaner-limbed babes feed. Like humans, some ewes are good mothers, some will be with a bit of help, some are feckless and only in it for the free accommodation.

While the lambs play in the sun, others work. Each ewe is fetched in, one by one, accompanied by her offspring. Lambs are checked for weight and health, and then the ewes have their care and maintenance: feet clipped and painted against footrot, backsides checked and cleaned, udders tested to see they are firing on both teats, and anything out of order found and corrected. Every single sheep is checked over in turn: backbreaking work. Some animals are co-operative, others infuriating, but they all receive the same level of care. Nor does it stop there.

I am not just here to admire the lambs and the work of the flockmaster. While the little ones race and play, and their mothers revel in the good spring grass, others wish to take advantage of the lamb-crop too. Sneaking through the stock-fence, lying flat behind the trees, waiting for an opportunity, come the foxes. How succulent a new lamb is for them: what a fine meal for growing cubs it will make. The foxes patrol constantly, for this is a curiously well-foxed area. In part, no doubt, this is due to incomers putting food out in their gardens. Foxes are attractive creatures, and many like to see them in their gardens, at least until the messes on the lawn become a trial, or the children's pet is taken from its hutch. However, the feeding of wild animals, while unwise because it causes artificial concentrations of them, may not wholly be responsible for the large numbers trading through.

A near neighbour has shot eighteen foxes in fourteen days. Other neighbours report steady success with traps and snares, while hounds and terriers on lambing-call have justified their existence every time they have come out. We in turn have an irregular but frequent presence with gun or dogs, to deter if we can and destroy if we must. And still the foxes come.

You can lure a fox into range of a rifle – some will come, many will not – you can set a snare or bait a trap with all the experience at your disposal, but if you actually want to find a fox, you must have the help of a dog. Nothing else will do that job.

So we leave the lambs and walk slowly through the fields, the dog questing all the time. Across the boundaries are fields all gone to scrub and weed; the owners live away during the week, and do nothing with the land, which is a perfect lie-up for foxes.

I send the dog in and he searches diligently, firing out a couple of roe deer, which do not concern us, briefly pausing and indicating an earth which was lately occupied but is no more, thanks to the trained terriers, then picking something up and retrieving it to me. It is a lamb leg, not that of a newborn lamb, but a sturdy limb from one several weeks old. Sighing, I pocket it to show the flockmaster later.

Together the dog and I work through all the areas of cover where we are allowed to go, checking under buildings and over stacks of hay and straw, finding evidence of foxes' passing but not the foxes themselves. There is one area of tumbledown sheds where we have not permission to go, and at which I would have liked a closer look. Maybe another time we will be able to run the dogs through there.

We head back through the big field, catching an unwary coney on the way, to report what we have found. The penultimate sheep sashays across the field with her new pedicure complete, and the last one, a sweet old girl of many years' acquaintance, waits obligingly for hers.

The shepherd and I discuss the lamb leg, and we arrange a night-time visit. Access to the sheds will be secured for next time we can come, with maybe a little extra manpower. The up-the-road neighbour would gladly lend his trap, but unfortunately people trespass on the land and have been known to smash up traps; strangely, these tend to be the same sort of people who say we should use traps in preference to dogs. There's no sense in it.

Well, we shall do whatever we can to help, by day and by night, and by all the legal methods available to us.

Happy and full of vigour, the lambs dance in the sunshine, neither knowing nor caring about the work and constant vigilance that underpins their existence.

Point-to-pointers and bluebells: the two have been inextricably linked in my mind for years, remembering when the season started two months later than it does now. Regularly and fairly hunted until January, the pointers would then enter serious training, and would, ground permitting, race until May. That meant some glorious mornings exercising through the bluebell woods.

Times change, and matters are different now, but this tiny yard still has point-to-pointers and bluebells. Though I no longer ride out on fit, fey Thoroughbred horses, I can still watch, and I remember how it was. The dog and I have climbed the hillside in the pre-dawn chill on business of our own, and now we rest among the short herbs and tiny downland flowers, our backs to a tree and our fronts bathed in the sunrise, out of the wind and perfectly comfortable. Below me, two point-to-pointers climb the track through the bluebells. Their hides, shorn to plush, gleam with health as the summer coat forces its way through what is left of their winter clip. As their quarters work, pushing them up the hill, their heads nod in balance, thin manes flapping on their necks, and low on their haunches the skin wrinkles briefly and then smooths with every stride. Under the neat hooves, the soil barely breaks, and their breath is white dragon-smoke through the dappled shade. The riders duck under the odd branch and then straighten, the thin morning air sharpening their hunger. They will be hungry until the end of the season, for they have weight to make which is below that which is natural for them, and muscle weighs heavier than fat, so the fitter they get, the hungrier they will be. The horses have no such worries: the art with these is getting them to eat enough. Sweet new greenery is calling them, but they are allowed only a tiny amount of this, and the rest is made up of high-octane fuel. After the season, they will have blissful days and nights at grass, but this is the time that they earn their future holiday.

Now the horses swing into trot, their limbs moving in diagonals, and I watch to see that the strides are even and forward-reaching. Heads and tails are carried high, and the skylark close to me sings so loudly that surely they must hear. The track broadens out and one horse moves upsides the other: now they will canter, and canter they do, along the good going, down the shallow slope, for horses must know how to

balance themselves on gradients, then where the ground pulls up for a sharp five furlongs, away they go, stride for stride together in a burst of serious speed. At the top, the riders sit up and slacken their reins; the horses slow down reluctantly, turn, and swing off out of sight, steam rising in the sunlight.

The dog and I stand and make for downhill. The horses, walking home, may well catch us up on the way, and I will be asked what I think, which is a courteous irrelevance, for my opinion is not the one that matters. The bluebells smell sweet in the morning, and will be sweeter yet at dusk, when the warmth of the dying sun is on them. Then, the horses will be warm in their rugs, crunching their food and dreaming of whatever it is that horses dream about, while the humans will be home to their one meagre meal of the day. The dog and I will be engaged on work of our own, back in the bluebell woods and out on the velvet hill, as the shadows grow long, and scent deepens with the dusk.

III

It was the chickens' alarm call that woke me. Normally at this time of year, the pre-dawn has me half awake and enjoying the song-thrush's melodic greeting to the new day as he perches unseen among the cherry blossom. Now this gentle start to the day was eclipsed by the strident blare of hens shouting for help. On the Richter scale of hen distress, this measured around a seven: cause for concern but not imminent death. Therefore I allowed myself the luxury of pulling on a pair of trousers before running outside; somehow one feels so vulnerable in less.

Accompanied by the usual assortment of dogs, I flung open the back door and saw my free-rangers surrounding an enormous rat. The hens sleep inside a well-fenced compound with some of the dogs. We have tried putting up perches, but on cold nights, the poultry prefers to sleep cuddled up to the doggery. When dawn comes early, the girls can stroll down to the official hen-house at any time that they wish, there to deposit an egg apiece and take the rest of the day at their leisure. Any fox scaling the static defences would be sure of the warmest of welcomes from the mobile ones.

No matter how securely you store your feedstuffs, you are never far away from rats. We prefer to use non-toxic methods of control, though sometimes, sadly, a big influx of them has to be poisoned. A few well-sited traps can catch steadily throughout the year, keeping numbers down adequately, but recent heavy rain and flooding has moved more rats into our area. I had no time to reflect on the origins of this rat, though, for while the hens held it at bay, the smallest lurcher dived in and caught it, despatching it with a crunch and a flick. He then retrieved it carefully, as he has been taught. I had no desire to handle this creature though, so I told him to drop it and issued him with a biscuit as consolation.

The hens continued to stare at the rat, making soft bubbling chirps to each other. Hens have a wide vocabulary, and are tremendous communicators. Not wanting them to eat the rat, which was clearly what they had in mind, I found the shovel and removed it, discovering as I did so that it was a heavily pregnant doe. This might have had those people unacquainted with the natural world in sentimental tears of woe, but my reaction was one of deep relief that we had got rid of the horrible creature before it had produced its young. Doe rats are barely out of nappies before they are pregnant, and are pregnant and suckling thereafter for the rest of their lives. That one rat which had died so swiftly could have been responsible for a mighty infestation if she and the buck that had impregnated her had been left. Any buck would do for her; father, sons, no problem. She would have littered over and over. But now she would enrich the compost heap, and we would likely catch a buck there within a day or two, hoping to devour the mortal remains of his erstwhile mate.

Very successful creatures, rats. Highly intelligent, marvellously adaptable, but you wouldn't want your daughter to marry one.

The dogs milled around with good-natured impatience as I fed the hens – brave girls! – completed the briefest of ablutions and put my clothes on properly. As we were up so early and had already had a successful hunt, they said, let us go out and see what else we can find.

I decided to take the path through the fields down to the stream: there might, after all, be another rat for us.

IV

Ten months old, this terrier pup, and thinks he's a big man. He's an old-fashioned sort of Jack Russell, no pretensions or Parsons, smooth-coated, short-legged, spannable, and slightly longer than he is high. He wasn't bred for any show ring.

What he is bred for is coming out quite naturally, as he has his walks with me. I am taking him out while his owner convalesces. You could not call it a chore: rather a constant delight. A lot of groundwork has gone into his training, so that he is well socialised, steady to cats, fowl and livestock, comes when he is called, and sits when he is told. I have put a little polish onto these accomplishments, nothing much, just some tidying, for he is now of an age where the hormones start to kick in and authority is challenged. Who are you to give me orders, he asks? I am your Uncle Foxglove, and we will have fine walks together, but no nonsense. Animals like to have clear demarcation lines, and he seems satisfied with the response. At any rate, we do not have nonsense, and in return, there are random titbits, caresses, and opportunities to do terrier things – with one exception. This little chap is too young to go to ground, but would very much like to. He has no knowledge of the Things that dwell under the surface, but they smell good. Being already master of mice and rabbits, he feels invincible, but I know better what can live down holes, and he is too young to meet them. Thus we must keep away from the wrong type of holes.

He progresses through the long grass in a series of leaps, like a little pied dolphin. Ahead of him, one of my old lurchers ambles, her pace casual, her instincts anything but. She drinks the wind, scans the horizon, smells the ground, and turns her huge dark eyes on me when she registers something of interest. May I go? says that look. I give her the signal and she breaks into her deceptive wolf trot that covers the ground so easily and yet looks so slow. Her small companion increases the length of his leaps to keep up, then dives sideways through the stock-fence into the stout hedge of mainly blackthorn. Satisfied at the way he is progressing, she stands on tiptoe, her tail curled for the take-off thrust in any direction a rabbit should bolt. Leaning on my stick, I enjoy watching their instinctive co-operation.

Rabbits scuffle about in the undergrowth. They won't go far, for they are well dug-in there. One bolts out of the hedge, sees the lurcher, whips round and back into the hedge and safety. Safety for now, that is, for as the little chap becomes more proficient, so he will have his mouth in the right place to capture a foolish bunny. He caught his first rabbit a few weeks ago, and is something of an expert on mice. But for now, the rabbits are safe, the old lurcher having little running left in her, and the stiffness in the joints that comes to us all, and the young whippersnapper with all of it yet to learn.

He bustles out again, and runs ahead of us to a place where the bury edges are just outside the hedge. With my superior height, I can see young rabbits spread out on their sides, sunbathing. Should danger threaten, they are mere inches from safety, and so completely relaxed. They should have a rabbit or two on guard, but they seem to have neglected this precaution. I wonder! The terrier pup has his nose down like a miniature foxhound, following scent, weaving across the grass in the wake of a rabbit that has run into covert several minutes ago: I know because I saw it. He runs heel, that is to say, where the rabbit came from rather than where it went, a common mistake in a young dog. But then he corrects himself, casts himself forward and picks up the scent going the right way. One or two of the sunbathing rabbits is sitting up now, for I am close enough for them to be concerned. Beside me, the lurcher presses against my leg and quivers. She would so like to run and catch one of these rabbits, but she knows that they would simply flip down their buries and be gone if she tried. She is too much of a professional not to realise this. Meanwhile, the terrier bowls steadily and accurately along the scent, following every twist and turn that his rabbit made, stopping where it stopped, and eating some of the droppings it left, then off again. If he lifted his head, he would see them, but he is following scent. Thus I have seen many times a fox run through a pack of hounds and emerge unscathed, because the hounds were intent on the scent. I have just as many times seen a fox run through a pack of hounds and not emerge at all, because one or two lifted their heads at the right time; just the luck of the game.

The rabbits are now watching us hard, and have their feet under them ready for when they have to jump. The lurcher and I have not moved, and the terrier has not raised his head. And now he is right at the buries, and the rabbits have all vanished underground, with nothing but a thump of hindlegs here and there to tell us that there were ever rabbits. The terrier is thrilled with scent, bustling all around the bury and sniffing ecstatically into the holes. I distract him before he thinks of trying to go down one, which he is almost small enough to do. I can tell you that he is made of the right stuff and it isn't easy!

Ahead of me, where I can see and the dogs cannot, is what looks like a patch of dock, lying rust-coloured against the yellowing green of the grass. But this is a tidy farm, not given to patches of dock. I watch, and presently, the weed twitches an ear very slightly. That is enough, and I summon the old lurcher with no more than a thought and a raised eyebrow. She is back at my side at once. I show her where to look, and she looks, but does not see at once, for the weed is still. But we have worked a long time together, she and I, and she keeps looking until the weed flicks its ear again. Then she is off, four unco-ordinated strides and then the adrenaline kicks in and overrides the aches in her old limbs. She flies across the grass as I remember she always did, head low, back arching and stretching, shadow ragged behind her and a little terrier blur behind that. The weed leaps into the air, sprouts a brush, and pelts through the five strands of barbed wire that make up the boundary fence just ahead of the dog. I stop her with one sharp, high call: I do not want her on the neighbouring land, and I certainly don't want her through the close-set wire. She comes back grinning and swinging her head from side to side: that was fun, she says. The terrier is smelling the smell where the weed had been lying, and as I don't want him through the fence either, I let him enjoy the scent for a few moments more and then set off back to find some more rabbits to distract him. He only hesitates a moment before he follows, showing the value of all the training his owner has put in. So much of training anything is timing and kidology.

The land shimmers with heat as we take the path back, butterflies all around us, and the little dog leaping through the grasses, being showered with pollen. Back at the house, he will snooze away the noontime in the company of his owner, all unaware that there are those trying to pass legislation to make his happy morning's activities a capital crime.

V

The storm had swept the footpaths clean, and dawn was just breaking as the dogs and I went over the stile into the first field. It was a lovely time to be out, well worth the small effort of leaving a warm bed. Dark lines through the silvered crop showed where animals had been, and the dogs feathered back and forth, tasting the scents as well as smelling them, snorting the water out of their noses. Everything seemed newly washed: goodness knows, we needed the rain, and more besides. Ground this hard in spring bodes ill for its state in the summer.

Pigeons were about, but not yet on the newly drilled peas. So was the pigeon shooter: I had seen him park in the farmyard and start to unload his equipment, which can be as simple or fancy as you like. This man is a traditionalist and as long as he has somewhere to sit and something to conceal him, that is enough. An elderly yellow labrador walked at his heels, delighted to have a morning out. His younger dogs would do a full day's shooting several times a week in the winter, but this pleasant old girl was past all that. These days, she was more than content to sit in a hide and do some retrieving during the lull between flights. Working dogs love to work, and it was good to see a caring owner who still found time to give his elderly dog a good quality of life. I noticed that he had not let her get fat, which is so important, especially with dogs like labradors which love their food, and undoubtedly this was a major reason for her still being so fit at her age.

The first of the Larsen traps was over here in the wheat, under a small tree which offered a tempting standpoint for the nest-robbers being drawn in by the call-bird. The trick is to use a call-bird from outside the local area, which so incenses the residents that they are unable to resist mobbing it. This bird had company, another magpie, which I removed and despatched out of its sight, a simple courtesy. Then I checked its food and water, which I had replenished the evening before, and left it in peace.

The last of the blackthorn blossom – late this year, and not much of it – was drifting, and the hawthorn leaves still drooping with newness along the hedgerows where I reached the second trap, empty apart from the call-bird. She too – I knew this one was a hen-bird – had plenty of victuals, and she looked at me with a bright, intelligent corvid eye, quite unafraid. She was a catcher of crows, notoriously difficult to trap, or shoot for that matter, and very valuable to the landowner for this reason. Whatever it was about her that brought crows in worked wherever she was sited. This hedge offered shelter and breeding space to a number of small bird species, and consequently brought in any number of crows and magpies, eager to wipe out eggs and nestlings. Thanks to this magpie and the Larsen, there would be fewer predators and more little survivors this spring. Similarly, birds such as skylarks, grey partridge and plover that nested in the fields would have a better chance to raise their young with fewer plundering corvids about.

I had one more trap to check, which took me through a flock of sheep with new lambs. The sun was well up by now, and the tiny lambs were uncurling and beginning to bounce. Baby rabbits, emerging from hedgerow buries, were just as delighted to feel the sun on their backs, and enjoying the sweet new grass. This pasture is rather rich for rabbits, which do better on dry coarse grazing, but the rabbit makes a living wherever it is born. The little ones dashed for cover as the dogs raced towards them, and, not being all that far from home, got there safely. The dogs came straight back to heel as they had been taught, ignoring the ewes and lambs. Sussex working dogs have to be totally reliable with livestock.

You look through the flock without realising that you do it, searching for anything amiss. No cast ewes, no dead lambs, everyone awake and looking bright. Shepherds will tell you that it is a sheep's ambition to die in any one of a number of imaginative ways, but they hadn't got around to deciding whose turn it was this morning, for which I was grateful. No foxes were about this morning, though I noticed a lingering peppery smell where one had marked by the hedge. The more eyes on the flock, the better, for foxes have all day and night to wait and find an opportunity to take a lamb. Nor do they just take small or sickly lambs, either, being well capable of killing strong, well-grown ones weeks after their birth. There is a fox trap hidden in the next field, and it has been busy in the last few weeks. I check it through binoculars, not wanting to get too close and put off any potential candidates, but it is empty and unsprung. Meanwhile, the dogs have run the hedgerows in the sheep field, and flushed nothing, which is good news for the flockmaster if rather disappointing for the dogs.

The third trap has caught another magpie, so not a bad tally since yesterday, for they are checked at dawn and dusk. Still with my magpie-handling glove on, I fill a carrier bag full of new nettles, taking care not to pick any with butterfly eggs on, and then add a good handful of goosegrass. This will be cooked and go into tonight's dog food, being very good for them. There is a patch of chickweed, which the hens will enjoy, so some of that goes into the bag as well. A couple of fronds of Queen Anne's Lace, just coming into flower, make the old horse very

happy as I pass his stable, and that is the end of the gardening. In the distance, I can hear the pigeon shooter getting started. My thoughts are on breakfast, the morning still new, the dogs well content and ready for sleep.

Foxes don't usually run across the middles of fields in broad daylight, not unless there is something predatory immediately behind them, and there was nothing behind this one. He looked a good big fox, probably a roving Lothario brought far from his own patch by the allure of a vixen. Most foxes would be paired off by now; perhaps he'd been unlucky. He was two fields away across the rife, concealed from the dogs by a strip of woodland, but easily visible to me as a splash of running russet across the bright green newness of the crop. Our walk would take us that way.

The year seemed all out of time. I had already seen baby rabbits clustered around the tree-stump bury, and two brace of tortoiseshell butterflies mating, pale from winter hibernation and brought out by a treacherous sun. They would be unlikely to live past the day, but how long is a sunny day if you are a butterfly? I hoped that they would be able to leave some eggs in a sheltered spot where they would survive. And yet here was a fox running across a field where it did not belong, late in the year to still be seeking a mate.

The dogs roved and quested, staying within shot as they have been trained, although I did not have a gun today. Scent was good, they told me. One was an old lady past her natural span, honourably retired with three dodgy legs, but still quality of life enough to keep her going. The other was slipping over the blurred line from prime of life to gently past his best, but not yet an old dog. The way the pair of them was working, you'd have thought they were both youngsters. A cock pheasant clattered skywards, calling his jagged cry, while the younger dog rocked back upon his haunches and looked to see if we were shooting today. No, the season has finished already, though it seems hardly a moment since it started. I reckon the pheasant knew.

Over the small bridge, then, and right-handed into the first field, where both dogs picked up fox scent, feathering like hounds, running a few paces heel and then putting themselves right, boring on forwards with that curious hitching canter that sighthounds have when they turn temporarily into scenthounds. It looked as if I was going to have to break into a jog to keep up with things, so I cut across the field to the gap in the hedge where I had seen bold Reynard run. There were long strips of standing water, for these fields lie low and are partly flooded for much of the winter, which makes them a good place for wading birds to find refuge. Through the same gap went the dogs, running with keen purpose now. And here, if you had eyes to see, you could see the cunning of the pack, even if the pack only numbers two, for the younger dog veered off to the edge of the field, while the old girl stood in goal.

Round the edges there were hump-backed stands of thick bramble, so old and closely intertwined that it seems as if a terrier would have trouble finding a way through. Into one of these the dog smashed, disregarding thorn and tangle, intent only on his quarry. Out shot the fox, with barely fifty yards of field to cross before he was back in cover, and the old dog gathered up her legs as if there were nothing wrong with them, took four massive strides to reach her fox, one more to get her balance right and then struck. As she did so, the other dog came pelting out of the bushes and latched onto what was now a dead fox. Adrenaline wearing off, the elder dog staggered a few paces and then lay down. While I was making sure that she was all right, her son shook the carcase, making sure that it was dead enough. They are chalk and cheese, these two: the old girl has always killed her fox and dropped it: the younger one likes to get more involved and gives the body a good shaking. The fox itself was not the biggest dog fox I have ever seen, but surprisingly heavy: I wished that I had the means of weighing him, but there is a limit to how much ironmongery you can take with you on a walk. I wonder what a fox has to eat to get that fat? You see, despite the baby rabbits we had seen first, there aren't that many around here because it is so wet. He was not a local fox, that was certain, because the area does not support them for long, and the landowners do not tolerate any fox presence in any case. Well, here was one less, and the farmer would be pleased because his wife's ducks would be safe for a little longer. I left the body by the gate, to be collected and incinerated later, and turned up the track to the house to deliver the good news. It was so well received that I came back with half a dozen duck eggs, and the dogs were given a piece of buttered toast each, with which they were every bit as delighted.

The grass verges are punctuated with young rabbits as I drive to the farm, which shows that my timing is good. Like the rest of us, rabbits like to come out and feed when the weather is good, and then retire to a place of shelter – I nearly said safety, but as I am on my way to see them, safety is a negotiable term. Growing rabbits eat proportionally more than grown rabbits, just as human teenagers seem to be bottomless pits. It is therefore important to deal with the new generation of rabbits as soon as it appears.

These fields were drilled not long ago, and a combination of light, steady rain and warm temperatures means that the crop has already struck. A light film of green shimmers over the wealden clay. These are hungry fields: I have been hunting over them for decades, and every year marvel that crops can be pulled out of them. Soon they will go over to permanent grazing, which I think will suit them better, but once they are raising cattle, I will not be able to keep after the rabbits all year round, as I do now. Cattle and dogs don't mix; moreover, cattle hooves poach the ground to the extent that a dog could injure itself badly if run on it, once the ruts have set. My dogs are safe with all livestock, but cattle will attack dogs, sometimes fatally. From next year onwards, I will be working these fields in winter only, when the cattle are off them.

Parking the vehicle in a safe and unobtrusive position, I pull on my boots, pick up my stick, and look with affection across the landscape below me. I may not own these fields, but I love them. Can you love land? I think so – people die for the love of it, after all. I know these fields in every season, in every type of weather: I know the wild creatures that live here, where they run and fly, when they come and go. By the time you read this, the cuckoos will have arrived, and I know where I will find a pair of woodcock. Soon there will be swallows and martins in the yard, which are welcome, unlike the collared doves which are there all year round. But the sparrowhawk will take a dove a day, which is her job, and let us hope she leaves the smaller passerines alone. So the doves do serve a purpose apart from being a pest to humans. I admit to enjoying their sleepy triple coo, but I like the throaty five-beat woodpigeon coo better.

The dog and I walk the fields in slow purpose, with her tacking hither and yon while I stride steadily, looking about me all the time. She does not know this land, so I let her work on her own initiative, marvelling at how often she is right by instinct where I am right from experience. She is young, a teenager herself, sometimes biddable, sometimes stubborn, overflowing with life and eagerness. Through the fence, over the brook to the rabbit buries; she essays to go into the neighbour's field but I check her with a word and a hand signal. She does not know the boundaries yet. As she runs back, a rabbit pops out of a gorse bank, and she whips around and nails it. She stands looking at me, rabbit in mouth, eyes showing indecision. Training says that she brings it back to me, and instinct says she eats it. You can see the battle going on in her lean head. I turn away and run, calling her, and after a moment of acute hesitation, she runs after me, dropping the rabbit at my feet and putting one of her long paws on it. Not the ideal presentation, but we have plenty of time for putting on the polish. How I take that rabbit now will colour what happens the next time she catches one, and for ever after. So there is a lot of praise, a deft sleight of hand, and bunny now dangles from my belt.

She seems to accept the decision, but she is a complex character, by no means the easiest dog that I have trained, and I take nothing for granted.

Two hours later, we are sitting in the lee of the hawthorn hedge, watching the shadows claim the day. I have five rabbits swinging from my belt, and I am very pleased with my young dog. I am drinking from my flask of tea, and she is mumbling over a handful of biscuits. She stretches out her lean body and rolls over, exposing a cream-furred pink tummy for me to rub, and shows me that tails wag almost as well upside down. It is a moment of deep peace and togetherness, such as you can only get with a working dog that is utterly fulfilled, and a human who understands these matters.

VIII

You might think that sitting in the garden with the newspaper and a cup of tea would be relaxing, and so indeed it ought to be. Morning work reaches a natural hiatus round about the time that tea or coffee and maybe a couple of home-made biscuits would fit in nicely, and it is doubly important to take advantage of this pleasantness in memory of all those occasions when it could not happen. Thus, mellow of thought, I looked around the garden, and it looked right back at me.

Take the patch that struggles to be lawn against a happy family of dogs and the odd hen. There is a frontier just across here, from the buddleia to the cherry tree, and a puff of black feathers shows that the cock blackbirds have, yet again, been disputing territorial rights. Their skirmishes are intent, fast and with no quarter given nor asked. The blackbird families have raised two clutches – Mama is feeding a newly-flown chick over by the gate – and will produce one more before the end of the breeding season, so that we seem to have a garden full of varying ages of blackbird. The younger fledgelings aren't too good at landing yet, and I nearly had one in my tea a few days ago. No doubt its parents gave it a good ticking-off for that.

Robins, now, these are supposed to be quarrelsome and pugnacious, but they actually seem to rub along quite amiably with each other. The older brood is just beginning to colour up about the breast, the younger still being speckled and with the juvenile yellow corners to their beaks. One mother robin looks like a bag-lady, feathers permanently awry from sitting on eggs – definitely not a Lady who Lunches – though the other three adult robins look reasonably tidy. One of these comes into the kitchen regularly, the dogs regarding him or her with amused tolerance. Outside, dunnocks, greenfinches, house sparrows and several varieties of tit come and go. It is charming to watch, even if you are better off to keep your teacup covered.

Near me at eye level prowl the ladybird larvae, which, like the honeybees, seem to be fewer every year. This garden has been organic for decades, and you would think we would have more. I ponder transferring the tiny black predators to the vegetable patch, where they would be doing even more good. A happy band of caterpillars romps in the nettles we have left for them, and some close relatives are playing Old Harry in the cabbages. Some you win, some you lose. No butterflies without caterpillars. The beans look good, though.

I am brought out of my musings by a loud clattering above me, and ample quantities of hawthorn tree falling all around. There are boundaries up there as well, you see. Two male woodpigeons are squaring up for battle, and within seconds, the brawl that ensues makes anything the blackbirds do seem pretty small beer. Pigeons might be soft and downy, might be exquisitely coloured in shaded pastels, might be a demanding target if you are shooting and a rich, glorious meal after you have shot, but they are also the avian equivalent of bare-knuckle fighters. They clout each other with hard blows of their wings, swinging, parrying, feinting and then delivering buffets and clouts, each trying to knock the other loose from his perch and sometimes succeeding. One will flutter onto the other's back to deliver vicious pecks to his head before his antagonist shakes him off and smacks into him with the full force of one wing. Feathers rain down from the tree, and a passing sparrow catches one in mid-air and makes off with it – feathering a nest, maybe? Or perhaps just playing? The woodies aren't playing, though, but deadly serious. One can imagine pterodactyls similarly engaged, millennia ago.

After a surprisingly lengthy exchange of blows, one pigeon crouches low on the branch, gasping, and the other manoeuvres to a branch above him, where he sits and bubbles out a series of coos so rich and deep that he seems in danger of splitting himself in two. That does it! The other pigeon rouses himself to a terrible fury, and despite the disadvantage of his position below the other, launches an attack so rabid that the supposedly victorious pigeon is left fluttering wildly to maintain his grip on the branch. Mrs. Pigeon, on her nest a few feet away, keeps her head down, and if she supports one or the other of the fighting cocks, shrewdly gives no indication.

Several things happen at once. As I notice the rest of the garden birds have fallen quiet, so a hen sparrowhawk rips through the trees sideways, the two fighting woodies parting and falling out of the tree with the classic woodpigeon clatter of alarm. She misses the pigeons but clutches a greenfinch in her foot, that I never even saw her catch, she was that quick. Mrs. Pigeon is flat on her nest, and the bird feeders are empty: the world has stood still for most of us and stopped for one.

Then it all starts up again, first the smaller birds ticking and pinking their stress, then the pigeons recovering their machismo and once again edging towards each other on one branch, bobbing their heads and raising their hackles. Presently the birds start feeding again, apart from the woodies who are, problem still not resolved, moving into battle once more. But my elevenses is over, and I must get on. Then I see that I, too, have been outmanoeuvred, for during the dramas of the last few minutes, quite a large dog has moved in like a stealth weapon, leaped upon the garden table and silently finished my tea and biscuits.

The tang of Rangoon oil and saddle soap dominates, but other less obvious scents invade from time to time. Newspaper and soft cloths are all around. Every now and then a dog sidles up and asks with penetrating eyes if something interesting is about to happen. This is a day for that timeless, enjoyable and necessary checking and mending of equipment.

The guns of course are stripped down, checked for pitting and other ills, and cleaned thoroughly inside and out. Leatherwork is saddle-soaped on gunslips, cartridge bags and bandoliers; game bags are cleaned and hung out to dry. Ferreting nets are hung up and checked with small repairs effected, while badly damaged ones are discarded after the rings, pegs and drawstrings are salvaged for re-use. I respray the wooden pegs with day-glo paint, so that I may find the nets more easily when they are set in thick cover. The smell of the paint is not anything like as pleasant as the other odours of the cleaning processes. Then ferret transmitter collars are thoroughly cleaned, the leather saddle-soaped, and the batteries of these and the receiver boxes checked and stored appropriately. The two carrying boxes are checked for loose fastenings, disinfected, and left open to the air as well.

There is nothing much to be done to the lamping equipment as it is used during the roughest of weather and therefore thoroughly dried and checked over each time. Winter walking boots are greased, laces replaced, and then put away; wellingtons that are beyond redemption are disposed of, and I promise myself as I always do that I will get a new pair before I need them. I get through two pairs every year and never seem to strike the right balance between comfort and performance.

Up and down the country, in countless gun rooms, tack rooms, garden sheds and back porches, the picture is similar. Fishing tackle is minutely checked and new flies tied, that which can be repaired is, and old faithfuls that are now past use are fondly bade farewell. Saddles, bridles and other harness are all stripped down and the leatherwork cleaned. Stitching is checked, metalwork polished, and the pile of equipment needing repair grows on the floor.

As the falcon moults in her mews, the falconer too is involved in

making new hawk furniture and mending the old, the coursing supporter oils the sets of slips and checks their cords for free running, terrier and hound couples are made good again, and in tweed, black, scarlet, moleskin and cord many a darn is effected, and buttons restored to their rightful places. As we work, we talk, for then the task is not work at all. And what we talk of is hunting past and hunting still to come.

Children learn names and ways and traditions, the old knowledge is protected for the next generation, who will do just as we are doing now for their own children and grandchildren. The beloved shades of Lady, Tess, Sandy, Teal, Wonder and Winsome gather to hear again the tales of their doing, our memories their immortality. It is no chore, this cleaning and mending of our fieldsports accoutrements, but part of our forebears and our future. Saddle soap, Rangoon oil and memories: joy that is yet to come.

X

Abdul Abulbul Emir and Ivan Skavinsky Skavar are not early risers; the first flush of greenfinches has been and gone before they emerge from the wood. Something the size of a cock pheasant trying to keep his balance on a bird-feeder designed for finches is a sight to behold: he sways and lurches, tail flipping up almost over his back, wing primaries standing out like fingertips in a vain attempt to stay on board until he has filled his crop.

To one side and below, Ivan Skavinsky is involved in a similar series of acrobatics as he creeps to the very end of the dead elder branch which will take him not quite to the other feeder. He must then stretch himself very long and thin in order to reach the sunflower seeds. Meanwhile, disgruntled finches have to sulk and twitter until the big gaudy fellows have finished feeding.

On the ground, their buff and brown hens scoop up the spilt seed and the handfuls of chicken corn that we throw out for them. We enjoy seeing the pheasants around: so do our hens, which flirt with the cockbirds. We have a freezer full of pheasants thanks to the bounty of the shooting season, and a garden enhanced by them as well, for these flamboyant birds would be unlikely to survive without humans controlling their predators.

Although Ivan and Abdul try each year to raise families with their respective harems of hens, few chicks reach maturity here, because they are outside the protection of the gamekeeper, having strayed from their shoot. In a few weeks' time, their friendship will be dissolved in a spate of dramatic fighting: they will stake out their territories and win their hens, and go their separate ways until autumn.

The small birds are pairing off too: all are appearing in smart new suits, and our nesting boxes are being inspected for suitability. Cock-fighting with human participation is rightly illegal, but cock-fighting the natural way goes on all around us at this time of year. Some birds have such territorial aggression that they ignore other dangers when they fight. It is not uncommon for a pair of battling blackbirds to be killed by the same cat, or to fly into a passing car, and I can personally assure you that a high-speed low-level blackbird up your shirt can make you fall off your bicycle.

Abdul and Ivan plummet off their precarious perches to go and join their hens, and the greenfinches return to the feeders. Pugnacious little things these are too, and few other species get a look-in until the greenfinches have thinned out. We can see a distinct flightline all the way from the far block of woodland.

A clattering of wings announces the arrival of the woodpigeon mafia, which gives road to few. They strut and preen in their grey double-breasted suits and talk business in rich low voices; meanwhile the more anxious collared doves have taken the place of the pheasant fiancées under the bird feeders. Robins, chaffinches, sparrows hedge and house, tits blue, great and occasionally coal, accumulate. This morning we had a pair of longtailed tits in as well, but they eschewed the vulgar crowd in the elder tree and instead partook of a more refined meal in the ambience of the apple tree restaurant. Now the blackbirds arrive.

And then a twittering and a scattering and a whoosh and thwack, and the sparrowhawk is suddenly there, upside down in the hedge with one savagely armed leg through the mesh of the fence. I am afraid that she is injured, and half out of my seat to go and assist, but luckily for us both

– an injured spar not being the most co-operative of patients – she extracts her yellow leg, pushes back out of the hedge, and goes to sit in the apple tree, which curiously is now quite empty except for her!

She stays for quite some minutes, giving me ample time to admire her beauty, until a visitor arrives, and off she goes as he opens the garden gate. The ticking of avian alarm calls subsides, and the bird feeders become busy again. I don't really want to be running a takeaway for sparrowhawks, but she has her place in the grand scheme, and only takes sufficient for her food.

Bird feeder traffic is slow and steady until mid-afternoon, and then the queues build up again. They have drunk a lot of water too – putting out clean water is just as important for them as keeping the feeders filled.

The glass is dropping: bad weather ahead, but you could tell without the barometer because the birds are coming in early to stoke up for the night.

And here come Abdul Abulbul Emir and Ivan Skavinsky Skavar with their good ladies, and I remember the song about their great contest, which has me smiling as I go about the afternoon's tasks.

XI

It was very very early. Thick dew silvered the grass so that my tracks showed as a ragged double line, and the lurcher made a single row of dots beside me that occasionally veered off as she checked a smell, or showed as a group of two offset pairs where she had stopped to view the distance. Fox tracks showed in a line like hers, but blurred from the drag of its brush, inviting her to tear along the dotted line, which of course she would have done if there had been a fox still at the end of them. It was half an hour or so gone, too long for us, only the rank scent still hanging on still air. A pheasant crowed not too far away, then another, and a magpie cackled.

Through the field of sheep, which was big and undulating with half a hedge in the middle that went nowhere, then the linseed field which would soon be a shimmer of blue in the folds of the land. Rabbits ran out of the crop all the way along. They don't like linseed but they still chew the plants down, maybe in the hope that it will taste better one day. The other side of the long narrow wood I could hear the 'keeper's quad-bike.

How many people realise what a guardian of the countryside the gamekeeper is? Every single day, and often at night too, he covers his beat over and over, sometimes on foot, sometimes by vehicle, seeing at once if something has changed. He manages a living theatre of habitat, scenery and acts changing constantly, but always within the same play. Old woodland, new plantation, cover crops, arable crops, livestock and ley, the land has to earn its owner's living in many ways apart from shooting. The farmer has one set of priorities, the shoot captain another, the books must balance and the pheasants must fly. But only the 'keeper walks the land by day and by night, keeping it alive. Everyone wants access, but the wild things must come first: blanket access disturbs wild creatures, crushes wild plants, can cause a myriad unnecessary deaths of fragile, rare or vulnerable life forms that could just as well flourish for the sake of a little understanding.

The 'keeper knows where the badgers are, and his constant vigilance defeats those who would do them harm. He knows where the buzzards nest, where the single pair of hobbies can be found, where the plentiful sparrowhawks hunt, but he will not tell anyone unless he has known them well for a very long time. What on earth motivates adults to do something as destructive and unnecessary as collect birds' eggs? He keeps these and other criminals away with his unpredictable patrols and superior fieldcraft.

The quad-bike appears, rounding the corner that the dog and I are approaching, and there is the man himself. "Heard you on your quad," I say. "Saw where you'd been," he replies with a grin. "I'll be finished in half an hour."

This means that we are welcome to intrude upon his brief coffee break: an honour indeed. Two sets of eyes are better than one, three if you count the lurcher, and I can tell him where and at what time I have seen foxes, whether they are young or mature, and any distinguishing features, for foxes differ greatly in looks. I see cartridge cases (he picks his up) I see dead animals and birds and can often tell what killed them, I see wires set, tyre marks, cigarette butts, all manner of things that convey useful information. In return, the lurcher and I are allowed to go where we wish, within the bounds of common sense and courtesy.

I take the remains of the charity balloon out of my pocket, the one that I picked up in the sheep field before a sheep could eat it and die. "That's not very Green, is it?" he says sadly, these balloons being such a nuisance to livestock and wild things. Then off he goes to finish his first round of the day before most people are even awake, guarding his acres which are safe haven for so many vulnerable creatures.

The lurcher bitch and I take the long way round to his cottage, to arrive after half an hour of making tracks in the silver dew, and sharing a red dawn with the silent secret tenants of the woods.

XII

Just a matter of weeks ago, when spring still hesitated on winter, I met a very special lady of great beauty. She stood on big yellow feet armed with scimitars of jet; you would have said her plumage was brown, or maybe you would have seen that it harboured every shade from buff to bitter chocolate, flowing through caramel, rust and umber. Her eyes were belladonna black and ringed with gold.

Like all creatures designed for function, she filled the eye. Her neat streamlined body was slung between legs as spare and muscular as a racehorse's, and reached up under her wings – such wings! Her tail could spread and close like a fan to balance them, and nothing there was of her that was not to purpose.

I was privileged to accompany her for a few hours with her team of helpers. These were a liver and silver coloured German shorthaired pointer, a tidy little polecat-marked jill ferret, and a tall man with the air of quiet authority that comes from living closely with the natural world.

The austringer's team is very different from the jolly, easy bonhomie of horse and hound. Neither hawk nor ferret can be directed in the way that social animals can, and such a triangle of hunters will tolerate rather than seek each other's assistance. Much work has to be done in training each to co-operate with the others, and the hunter holds in his hands the delicate threads that link but do not bind the three. Man has ever had the skills to tip the scales a little, and this is why today we were fielding a Harris hawk, probably the most tolerant of the shortwings, and with the advantage that, in the wild, they hunt in family groups. Thus she would have slightly more inclination to be part of a team, and less likely than, say, a goshawk, to have a fit of the vapours in the presence of a strange human. In fact, although she was clearly extremely eager to go hunting, she was also quite genuinely pleased to be in our company, and had no intention of letting her owner out of her sight.

Once we were in the woods and she was released, she flew from tree to tree after us, her bells tinkling, watching us closely. We found a likely bury and the dog marked to show us that rabbits were at home.

Down went the ferret, and we all waited. The dog sat staunchly, knowing that his part of the job was done and that he must not chase any rabbit that bolted. The Harris sat above us, seeing so much more with her raptor's eyes than we would ever see. After some preliminary underground rumblings, a rabbit pelted out of the bury, the man gave the centuries-old falconer's cry, and the hawk streaked in and out of the trees, turning more tightly than you would have believed possible after the twisting, jinking rabbit. It was a thrilling burst of flight, even though the rabbit reached the safety of another bury before the hawk could catch it. A jingle of bells and a rousing of feathers above us showed that she was back already to wait for the next one.

Being late in the season, the ferret had to work extra hard to evict any rabbits, meaning that both dog and bird had to show great patience. We tried other buries and moved a few more rabbits; the afternoon became warm and the Harris indicated that a bath would be appreciated at the same time that the ferret showed us she too was beginning to tire.

It is incumbent upon the hunter to put the needs of his animals first, so we agreed to call it a day. The ferret was put back into her carrying box, and a delighted hawk plunged into a shallow part of the stream that she had been eyeing for some time. She had a blissful bath and then climbed out, looking like a collection of wet rags on feet that seemed to be several sizes too big. A wet hawk cannot fly, of course, so she clambered onto a low branch to wring out and fluff her feathers, and stepped from thence onto the proffered gloved hand of her owner.

Though her flights had been unsuccessful, she and I had much enjoyed our trip out. On our return, after setting the animals fair, we had a cup of tea and watched some incredible film footage of golden eagles being flown to foxes and wolves in Mongolia, and red-tailed hawks working squirrels in America.

A bird of prey is a huge commitment, and one to which I could not do justice, but thanks to the young man who gave up half a day to show me the bare bones of a hawking team in action, I was able to experience this marvellous field sport at first hand. And, as has always been the reaction when I have taken people to see my own activities, the response is: "That was wonderful – when can we go again?"

XIII

The lowering pressure meant a night that would be wet and windy, and the moon was less than a quarter. The day had been something that could not pass quickly enough. The dogs knew, and the ones that would be left behind burned their gaze reproachfully into me. One lucky lurcher, small, neat, all muscles and ribs, bounded into the vehicle with us.

There would not be many more nights like this, with the weather and the moon just right, the going soft but not too heavy, the crops high enough for a rabbit to sit and think itself concealed, too high for a dog to see but not too high for people. The wind smelt warm and good, the cloud cover seven okta, seven-eighths of the sky. Dog and we turned our faces to the wind, and that part of all dogs and all people that is forever hunter flooded us with adrenaline and race memory.

Can you go quickly without hurrying? Can you move quietly without tarrying? So the three of us crossed the footpath, walking under the glow of the new housing estate, then by the woods and the old farm buildings, to where the direction of the wind and the lie of the land made our best start.

Flick on the lamp: flick off. That tiny interval of light told us much: rabbits out by the pond, fox in the hedge three hundred yards away and wrong for the wind, fallen branches close in that should not be trodden upon. No need for words when we all three shared one mind, which is the way of a good hunting team.

There we were, abeam the feeding rabbits: pick one, send the dog.

The dog is true to the beam. Though she cannot see from her height, we can see from ours, and she works on trust. The rabbit is away and so are all its friends, but the dog does not chase harum-scarum, as an untrained one might. Only one rabbit is hers, and that is the one in the beam, the one making for the bury in the hedge, except that she will not let it. She overtakes the rabbit and runs beside it, goalkeeping it away from refuge. The rabbit turns and turns again, gaining ground from the dog, which spins around after it. The soft soil favours the rabbit, but not much; behind the lamp, the work is to keep the rabbit in the beam but not the dog, and not to get in the way of either.

The rabbit is looking behind as much as before it, and rabbits have been known to run straight into lampers. This one leaps clean over the head of the dog and races for the bury, reaching it a snap ahead of its pursuer. Keep the lamp on: rabbits tumbling into holes where they do not live are often forced out again straight away by the rightful residents.

Not in this case, though. Lamp off: dog returns straight away, for so she has been taught. A good healthy sporting rabbit survives, nothing more than a little breathless, as is the lurcher. When she has her tongue in again, we flick the lamp on to see if any rabbits have opted to sit tightly rather than run in, and one has done exactly that, but a good way away.

We walk quietly in a semi-circle to approach it from a better angle, and put the lamp on again. Yes, it is still there. Only the light reflecting off the inside of one partly-raised ear gives it away. If both ears were tightly down, the rabbit would stay sitting: one ear up indicates that this rabbit is on its toes and ready to run. So is the dog, who is up on it very quickly, fast enough to snatch it off the ground before it has taken more than a couple of strides. That's this half of the field empty, except for the fox which is following at a discreet distance.

We pass the buildings just far enough away so that we will not suddenly be floodlit by the security lights, and make for the top of the field, which gives us two more runs and one more rabbit. The next field involves negotiating a metal gate, which makes more noise than I would like, but luckily the wind is gusting hard and disguises most of it.

Here the dog picks a rabbit neatly out of its seat and then, over-confident, loses the next one by miscalculating its intended direction. That makes her concentrate better, and the following run is pure poetry, evasive action and counter-ploy, the dog really using her brain, and a lovely catch at the tiny moment of hesitation that a rabbit makes before it goes through a hedge. One day, this dog will be very good indeed.

We cross the brook at the shallow part, and run the two big fields in the lee of the wood, which, as you would expect, have more rabbits in them than are in the colder fields. The fox looks back at us from the housing estate, where it probably goes to scavenge good pickings from the rubbish bags left out for tomorrow's refuse collection.

Our game bag is warm and heavy with rabbits, and the dog has done enough. It is a pity that the fox was wise to us, but a proportion of them always will be, and there will be others less canny at another time. You cannot shoot safely over the fields that we have been working because of the proximity of the houses, so the dog is invaluable. We have passed within a few yards of the houses on occasion, but disturbed no-one.

As we walked back to the vehicle, a beautiful barn owl wafted across in front of us, and we watched her wraithlike swooping flight as she skimmed the hedgerow, hunting her own dinner. We had not disturbed her, either.

XIV

Fox in the henhouse is a cliché, but the results, once seen, are never forgotten. Headless hens scattered wherever you look, little piles of hen bodies in the corners and under the nest boxes where they tried to hide from the red terror, feathers, feathers everywhere, never in the world would you have believed there could be so many feathers.

Four living hens we find, deeply shocked, four left out of seventy. They will probably die as well, but we find them warm quarters with just enough light to see their food and water, squirt a herbal remedy for shock into each beak, and leave them huddled together. The problems are only just starting for my friend, who depends on the money from her free-range flock to make the difference between solvency and debt. She is a downsizer from the city, who has taken her redundancy pay to fulfil the dream that many others have too: the organic self-sufficient environmentally-friendly smallholding. In the words of the song, there'll be a load of compromisin' on the road to her horizon, but she has given it her best shot, and I admire what she has managed so far.

Total self-sufficiency is impossible nowadays, but if you are willing to work very hard for long hours just to break even, then you can come close. But it is the devil of a learning curve. I knew her when I, too, worked in that city; I, the hunting, shooting omnivore and she the disapproving vegetarian, both of us keen environmentalists but approaching the same world from opposing directions. Ironically, I was the person she contacted when disaster happened, and naturally I came over straight away. I asked if it was all right to bring one of the dogs, and she said of course. I left the vehicle at the gate and walked up past the farmhouse to the scene of carnage.

We gathered up the bodies of sixty-six good young laying hens, and took them to be incinerated. Well, almost all, because to my surprise she asked if we should keep some back for bait. She who had always railed at me for my fox-killing activities had just become a confirmed vulpicide. So we dug the hole, gathered the wood and made a pyre of sixty-four of them. With a larger property, I could have baited the middle of a field for a couple of nights, and then sat in wait with the lurcher, for this land is unsafe for rifle shooting. But the dog is limited here in where she can go, and if she were to pursue a fox onto the neighbour's land – another vegetarian downsizer – it would not have been well received. Therefore we would have to use lesser methods.

First having attended to the survivors and the funeral, we had to find where the beggar had got in. This was another job for the dog, my good old bitch who was such a remarkable foxer in her youth. She knew what was wanted, and cast around the farmhouse until she picked up the scent that led to where Charles James Fox had scraped a hole right under the dug-in wire, a hole by which you would have thought not even a rabbit could have entered. A fox scat had been left by way of signature.

If I had brought the terrier, she might have rolled in that, unsavoury little dog that she is. How had it got into the run? I looked around: the run seemed impregnable, but I know of foxes climbing wire, and maybe this was one such. The electric wire around the base of the pen had not deterred it. This lady, who had often assured me in her city days that it was careless farmers who had their stock taken by foxes, and that they would have been all right if they had shut their animals in properly, was visibly shaken.

"It'll come back in the daytime: you know that?" I told her. Until she had started with her holding, she had thought that foxes only came at night. Steadily losing fowl during the day she had borne bravely, saying that she did not mind losing one or two if there were cubs to feed. But she had lost thirty in a few weeks, and now the others, bar four, were gone as well. With them went much of her ready cash, which, with the closure of so many village banks, meant that she would have to drive into the town and pay for parking just to cash a cheque for her everyday needs. Restocking would not be an option until the fox had been killed, but even so, you cannot just go into a hen shop and buy another hundred fowl. They must be ordered and waited for; when they come, they will be point-of-lay, producing tiny unsaleable eggs to start with, some even without yolks. Within a few weeks, the eggs would be good but small, while the pullets would be growing fast and eating large amounts of the expensive organic food that she gives them. These eggs, while delicious, are not popular with most buyers, who prefer large ones. Even supposing we killed this fox within the next couple of days, it would be four months before she could equal yesterday's egg money, and she still had to pay for the new flock.

Then there were the remaining hens, which would need somewhere else to live if they survived, for you cannot put hens in a new flock. Chickens are extremely aggressive, and they would be set upon and killed, which fact I am even now having to explain to a kind person who thought that they would all be friends together. After years of pooh-poohing my comments, this lady has at last realised that I had been talking sense all along, and she accepts this new piece of information with that understanding.

Meanwhile the dog has followed the scent to the hedge by the road, which has a run showing through the early growth of grass.

"You could put a wire there," I say, and brace myself for the explosion.

"You mean a snare?" she says, white with resignation. I nod.

"You'll come straight away if we catch it?" Of course I will. I hate seeing trapped foxes, but sometimes these things have to be done.

Before I leave, I have set a wire in the hedge and hidden a cage trap in the hen run. This is baited with one of the deceased, and we have already established that no, the fox will not be taken and released anywhere else, because that would be immoral – nobody needs a poultry killer nearby, and a fox released on another fox's territory is going to suffer.

Coffee in the farmhouse is a glum affair, and I feel great sympathy for this brave woman who has seen so many cherished ideals crumble in the face of reality. "I still don't agree with hunting," she says to me.

"First come and see the lurcher at work," I tell her, knowing that the speed and efficiency of the lurcher will pave the way for greater understanding in the role of the dog in fox control. "Then think about coming foxhunting with me one time next season, and I'll explain exactly what is happening."

She didn't say no. And she did ask me to write this.

SUMMER

I

A promise to a child is not to be made lightly, for it must always be kept. For his birthday dinner, this youngster could choose any one of a score of popular dishes, but to all our surprises, what he has chosen is not a pizza or a burger, or anything else that you might expect. He has been reading some of my old country books, and is always interested in my tales of how things used to be. He wants rabbit pie. Not just any old rabbit pie, you understand, but one that we have made together, from scratch. Which means, first of all, that we must catch a rabbit.

And that is why yesterday, he, the dog and I were walking the hedgerows at dusk, through the clouds of zithering midges, trying to find the sort of rabbit that would grace a pie. The crops were high enough to conceal a rabbit, unless it sat up and showed the tips of its ears, and the dog was using his nose to try to find them. Every now and then he would stop, paw raised, head cocked, trying to pinpoint the position of a rabbit that he could smell. How better to catch a rabbit than by using a dog?

We could, of course, have set a snare or a trap to catch a rabbit in our absence; on other ground we might have shot a rabbit, but the layout of the farm and the height of the crops made that difficult now. The time for ferreting was over, now that lush undergrowth writhed over every bury. But a dog – you can use a dog all year round and in almost all conditions.

By the time our walk around the farm was complete, and a solitary blackbird poured evensong into the gathering dusk, we had three rabbits suitable for our task. They were young ones, promising to be sweet, tender eating. Together we paunched, skinned and cleaned them, then jointed them and put them to soak in salted water. We had more than enough for a rabbit pie, but rabbit pie is also good eaten cold, and I thought some might be taken to school in the lunchbox. The rabbits would soak overnight, and I would call next morning for the making of the pie.

Normally, neither this child nor I would be seen at a supermarket, but we had a long shopping list. With both parents working all day, little food was cooked from scratch at his house, and so there was not much in the cupboards to suit our purpose. Therefore we bought flour and fat, vegetables and herbs, and rushed back, all excited, to make our pie. Luckily, I still have my mother's old pie-dish, big enough to make a rabbit pie for a family, for the boy's mother had nothing in the way of pie dishes at all.

We had rinsed off the rabbit meat and set it to cook slowly with a beef bone before we left, and so on our return we drained off and saved the cooking liquor, and put the meat out to cool. Then, after washing our hands unusually thoroughly, I gave directions and the lad made his first ever pastry.

Next, while this was 'resting' in the refrigerator, we prepared the vegetables: mushrooms, celery, turnip and swede, cut up the bacon pieces, added the herbs and some seasoning, and thinly sliced a Bramley apple. I showed him how to take the rabbit meat off the bones, being careful not to miss the floating ribs, and next we chopped the liver and kidneys finely. Then all was mixed up with a little stock, the pastry was rolled out with a certain amount of apprehension and my mother's marble rolling pin, the dish lined and filled, and I showed him how to put the pastry lid on and crimp the sides. Last of all, we re-rolled some of the left-over pastry snippets and made a rabbit to go on the pie-crust. We glazed the whole crust with beaten egg and milk, and then put our treasure in the oven.

Then we had a big clean-up of the kitchen so that we would not get into trouble!

It certainly gives you new respect for those mothers of yesteryear, who would cook like that every day, with nothing but the range and old stone sink by way of appliances. We still had the potatoes and vegetables to prepare, but the pie would be a while cooking, and we had both had enough of domestication by then. His mother had promised to bring a pudding home – we had asked for something light to follow that big pie! – and so we did not have that to concern us.

What better way could there be, then, for us to throw off the shackles of the kitchen than to wake up the dog, drive to the farm, and see what we could find along the hedgerows?

II

The year is moving on: the dawn chorus is less intense, and the first fledglings from our garden blackbirds and dunnocks have already flown. The rabbits still need attention, though, and so I am on the edge of the woodland at dusk, waiting for them to appear for their evening feeding. The day has been wet and stormy, and I estimate that they will not have fed earlier because of this.

Against a pellucid sky, a single bird flies, muttering its soft nasal chuckle, a long bill pointing downwards. He is a roding woodcock on his territorial patrol. These woods always have woodcock in the season, and though we are on the very edge of their breeding range, several pairs nest here, a gift every year. I like to see these charming birds about. An intense churring from further into the woods tells me that the nightjars are here as well. In contrast to the appealing woodcock, the nightjar seems sinister. It is a large untidy bird, silent in its flight like an owl, and with the ability to throw its voice, for though you might hear the call, you would be lucky to see the bird itself if you followed it. Yet sometimes you will see the big, barred feathers on another bird in a different tree, and it takes a moment to unite the voice over there with the bird over here, by which time it will likely have hidden itself and gone quiet. As you ponder, you will hear the churring start up again somewhere else.

There will be a lot of moon tonight if the sky stays so clear, and if we get more cloud cover, the chances are that it will bring another storm with it. We do not, therefore, have the best of nights for shooting, but will do what we can. The dusk deepens into silver and black with a single carmine streak above the downs, and the first rabbit drops to the gun. We walk as silently as it is possible for a human to walk, footfall before footfall, rocking on the balls of our feet before each step. Pause, take the weight in balance, shoot. Though the ground is wet, wellingtons make too much noise, so we each wear leather boots, and walk carefully so that the ground sucking away from each step does not give us away. Fortunately the tracks are well mossed between the tyre-marks of the forestry vehicles. On occasion, a mis-step causes a twig to snap, or a squelch, though not necessarily detrimental to our cause. Sometimes a rabbit will sit up and swivel its ears in the direction of the unexpected sound, and offer a better target. A roe deer catches the whiff of us, whirls and dashes into the woods. Just inside the treeline, she pauses to bark and stamp at us, annoyed rather than frightened. She is extremely fat, and will be dropping her twins soon.

By nightfall proper, we have eleven rabbits and one wet foot between us. Now we go by vehicle, and noise is no longer an issue. There are fields that we normally lamp but which are too wet today, so we do not have all that large an acreage to cover. It is in the next brace of fields that we shoot the first of several rabbits with myxomatosis. This disease is normally about in autumn, but another mild winter means that it is stirring again with the warmth of the spring. Spring 'myxy' often hits harder than autumn, because it is spread by the rabbit flea, and the flea population finds it easy to increase in the warmer months. If a doe rabbit has 'myxy' and survives, she will pass a temporary immunity to her young, but this will wear off before they can breed at four months old. Therefore, if the disease takes hold in the new breeding stock, the rabbit population will struggle to recover. This is good news for the landowner but rather less good for me, because I rely on a plentiful supply of rabbits to feed my own animals. Well, it can't be helped, and we will continue shooting because myxied rabbits still eat and cause damage. It is a quicker and more humane death for them in any case if we shoot them, even if we cannot use the meat.

Young rabbits are in good supply, though testing targets for their small size. They may not yet run as fast as a grown rabbit, and they are not wise to the lamp, often pausing where a more experienced rabbit would run, but there is not a lot to aim at. Each one makes a ferret snack, or a meal for the magpies in the Larsens. Like all young growing things, baby rabbits eat proportionately far more food than adults. Teenage rabbits are superb eating for people, too, the traditional way being to joint them and fry them in butter.

Over in the yard, eyes glow green. Two eyes, which means a predator, for herbivore eyes are to each side of the head so you can only see one at a time. Cat or fox? Or maybe a stray dog? You must be sure before you take the shot. Fox, I think, because the owner of the eyes turns aside and runs the hedgeline. We try a squeak to tempt him in, but he's having none of that. Too many people shoot foxes around here for him not to be suspicious.

Twenty-eight rabbits: not a huge amount, but still worth the effort. Rain sprinkles the windscreen as we climb the hill, and then as we level out at the top, there is – what is that sound?

Switching off the engine, we listen entranced. A nightingale, the first I have heard this year, is giving his all in song. Such an undistinguished little brown bird: such a glory of voice. He sings, we listen, and the world pauses.

III

The telephone call was almost in shorthand – farmers don't waste words. 'We're cutting the hundred acre tomorrow."

Three of us come with guns, to walk with the combine. Where you walk depends on the wind direction: harvesting is a hot and gritty business at best, and you don't walk downwind of all the dust and debris thrown out by the combine. If circumstances allow, we have one gun slightly ahead, one alongside, and one well to the rear, which covers most eventualities.

In the horse-drawn days, fields were harvested from sides to middle, and when there was an acre or so left to cut, standing alone in the middle of the field, all the local men and boys and cur-dogs surrounded it and killed the bolting rabbits as they fled from the reaper. Nowadays we harvest from one side of the field to the other, and instead there is a steady trickle of departing wildlife rather than one mad dash at the end. Indeed, the last two rows cut are generally empty, but we are always ready in case something has tarried too long.

Mostly our quarry is rabbits, though there might be foxes to thin out as well. We know where the fox earths are, and although the foxes have been living above ground in the standing crop for these many weeks, as the cover starts to diminish, it is towards these earths that they run. So we know from where and to where the foxes are likely to break, and are placed just so to intercept them.

The rabbits exit several ways. Some go hell for leather to the buries on the far boundary, which is where the combine cut its first row. As they cross the no-man's-land of stubble, they provide a sporting shot. Others, leaving the protection of the standing crop, squat in bewilderment at the unexpected change in their scenery, and are picked off easily. Rabbits bolt under the combine and out again, some getting badly maimed until the killing shot ends their pain. Some sneak across the stubble, ears flat, body flat, and don't begin their run until they are well clear of the noise and machinery. These are picked off efficiently by the back gun, who also accounts for a stoat which is bouncing across the rabbit buries. A squeak makes it sit up and offer a good target, and over it goes. A handsome creature in russet, with a white chest and black tail-tip, he is most unwelcome where scarce ground-nesting birds are trying to re-establish, and his death will make all the difference to them next nesting time.

For this job, safety rules are vital, and only the safest of guns are allowed to walk with the combine, unlike the free-for-all of bygone days. Our group has seen a good few harvests together, which is why we get that telephone call, the farmer knowing that we will do his job well without taking risks.

A few hours in the blistering heat and dust starts to feel like hard work, but we took over three hundred rabbits off this field alone last year, and that was just the beginning. A series of nights on the new stubble with lamp and rifle accounted for nearly as many again, and then we went in with the ferrets. Even so, there were still enough rabbits to keep the lurchers in business, once the rain had softened the stubble enough to make it possible to run them, and all these rabbits were spared the long agony of death by myxomatosis that follows the wet days of every autumn. Overcrowding and stress weakens rabbits to the point where this awful disease cuts swathes through them, and never is this better seen than on land close by, where rabbit fencing is used. Very efficient at keeping rabbits out, this forces them into unnaturally high concentrations, where shortage of food, build-up of parasites and the trauma of a population density that is far too high condemns them to a lingering death. Luckier by far are the conies that, fleeing the roar of agricultural machinery, roll over to the gun in the heat of the harvest, as the dusty ballet of combine and grain-cart and three walking guns works to safeguard your daily bread.

IV

Wooden gates are altogether nicer to see and to lean against, as well as much more inviting to set a hunter at when hounds are running. Metal gates, however, require less maintenance, and so what you see nowadays are more and more metal gates on farms. Metal gates also make a noise when you open them, which is a nuisance if you happen to want to be quiet as you go through the fields.

It is around ten in the morning, and already far too hot. I am on my way back from a pleasant visit to a farmhouse, and have been asked just to take a look at the sheep as I am going that way. The more eyes cast over the flock at any time, the better. This flock compromises an assortment of ewes with well-grown lambs, some decorative, some practical, and all very friendly. The gates groan as I struggle with the metal bar that opens and closes them: the hinges cry out as they swing. No danger of not attracting attention here.

There follows much bleating, and a small group of sheep surrounds me and the dog. Other sheep, more worldly-wise, know that I do not represent food, and stay lying down in the shade under the trees or under the hedge. They all seem to be the right way up, which is what you look out for when you are casting an eye over the sheep on a casual just-passing-through sort of basis. The walking ones aren't limping, and the lying-down ones are all breathing. Here and there a lamb lies flat-out in the sun, but betrays its continuing survival with a flick of an ear. All seems to be well.

Down the hill, another group within the flock is grazing. The sun makes every fleece look yellow, and a long thin yellow sheep is walking in an unsheeplike manner through the others. The gait in fact is very foxlike, and squinting against the sun I see that what I am looking at is not a skinny yellow sheep but a large yellow fox.

There is a wide variety in colouring in red foxes, from almost black to pale fawn, leucistic, which is creamy with darker markings, and albino, as well as the customary bright russet. This fox is very nearly at the limit of my eyesight, seeing as I am not wearing my spectacles, but I can still see what she is doing even if her edges are a trifle blurred. She is quite unconcerned about my presence. She knows that I am there because of the noise I made getting through the gates, because of the bleating of the sheep when they came up to me, because I am standing on the ridge, and because the wind is behind me, blowing the scent of human and dog to her. She can see me, smell me and hear me: just a moment ago, I was speaking to the sheep as I walked by them. If she is not afraid of me, she should be afraid of the dog, but she is not bothered by either of us.

I, by contrast, am very interested in her presence, especially as, I am told, she often has two cubs with her. No sign of these today. This time of year, cubs are hunting for themselves. In fact, studies have shown that at a mere twelve weeks old, when puppies are still very much babies, fox cubs are catching birds and animals. These cubs are quite a bit older than that, and the vixen has been bringing them close to human habitation, and teaching them things that foxes are better off not learning. Wild foxes tend to be a lot shyer than this: I wonder why she is so bold?

I watch her picking about in the grass, scrunching up a beetle here and there, fossicking in the dung piles. I summon the dog with a snap of my fingers: she pricks her ears at the sound and looks straight at me. She should have run then, but no, apparently satisfied that it is only a human and a dog, she continues searching the ground.

She is a good hundred yards away and right by the stock-fence: she would be through it in a flash if I sent the dog. With him at heel, I walk towards her. She sits and has a good scratch. I close to fifty yards; she sees me approach and cares not one jot. There is something not quite right about this fox.

The dog is quivering at my side. It is unfair to send him: he cannot possibly catch her. Once through the fence, she will be in the scrubland of the neighbour's untended fields, and into one of the earths there. She looks at me again, and carries on with her mooching. I send the dog.

He is past his prime but still fast and determined, and he closes the distance running hard. The vixen stands and stares at him. Just a dog running, so what? She continues to watch with what seems to be mild contempt as he gets within a length of her, then belatedly realises that perhaps she should run, but she is too late.

She turns out to be an expensive fox, for the dog has cut his foot and split his nail on one side, and grazed both of his stopper pads from the handbrake turn that it took him to connect with her. He will be off work for six weeks or so. She will not be teaching her urban ways to her cubs any more, and it can be hoped that, without her influence, they will keep away from houses, and more importantly, the poultry. That is, unless someone has been feeding them in their garden. We will see what happens.

Meanwhile, my dog needs a drink and a little first-aid. The metal gates shout to the world that I am going through them again, the sheep graze or cud contentedly, and the sun shines impartially on all of us.

V

Ancient broadleaf woodland, older than Sussex itself. Silver and gold moths flit around me, centuries of sharp-grassed turf and soft moss cushion my footfall. I am here as a guest in the dusk: my colleague carries a noise-moderated rifle.

When you walk the crepuscular hours, you link with thousands of generations of hunting ancestors. Senses become acute as twilight fades colours to monochrome. Scents take the place of primary colours and you become aware of the warm leafmould odour rising and spreading in the cooling air. There is thunder about; a short, heavy shower brings out the smells of the different trees, as distinctive as their shape. The air tastes metallic.

A bat flies around us, creaking its rusty-hinge squeak. Looking up at him, I almost collide with a stag-beetle, which sees me in ultra-violet and therefore barely at all. Bats and stag-beetles tell us that this landowner has left dead trees standing, to provide homes for these and other small creatures, for tidiness is death to wildlife.

This sporting estate is run on organic principles, and I was turning my feet at every step to avoid tiny flowers and insects. Grey spires of orchids watched me from beneath their brows.

We walked as hunters walk, a pace like a slow march, rocking from one foot to the next, avoiding noise from dead leaves and twigs. Such is the compulsion of the age-old instinct that we took care not to leave footprints, though there was no need. What atavistic enemy might have been tracking us, millennia ago?

Yet you cannot suppress your own scent, and a roe doe broke cover before us. She stopped, and stamped, and barked her disapproval before bounding out of sight. She barked twice more, getting further away, working round in a circle to get behind us. Roe were not our quarry this time, though the woodpigeon that clattered off in her wake might have been. A magpie rattled a curse at us: definitely on the quarry list, and knowing it.

My companion signalled to me to wait back. Well, he may have signalled or it may have been hunters' telepathy. Two rabbits waited on the ride to our right, though neither of us could see them for the moment. The man with the gun flowed to his knees, then lay outstretched. Fluid as the long shadows, he rocked back into a crouch, up onto his feet and rejoined me smiling, shaking his head. A careful man, he never shoots unless he is sure of a kill.

We went on through the wood and my friend shot a rabbit, then another, on the broad rides of spiky grass. As the dusk deepened, the birdsong poured around us, interweaving like the ribbons on a maypole. Softly he breathed a single word: "Nightjar".

I have heard the nightjar's song memorably described as 'like a pneumatic drill in a paper bag'. As we walked along the track, the churring became deafening until, surely, we were under the very tree in which they were sitting? But we could not see them until they took off in a ruffle of barred feathers, to resume drilling in a paper bag in a different tree.

The sky was black now, part with thunder, part with night, clouds scudding the half moon. Another rabbit taken, then another. Now owls superseded the songbirds, and a pair of buzzards mewed with delight as they played tag around the trees before retiring to bed. Sometimes you could hear the nightingale, I was told.

I was not lucky enough that time, though perhaps I could come and listen to the nightingale another evening. The remaining light turned yellow, then lightening crisped the sky and penny-sized raindrops started to bounce off us. We reached the vehicle, reluctantly shedding the senses of the hunter to protect ourselves against the petrol fumes, headlights and noise of the journey back to what some might consider civilisation.

VI

Somewhere in the back lanes of West Sussex, I was not lost, you understand, but in pilots' parlance 'temporarily uncertain of position'. Someone had been conducting a programme of vandalising the signposts, which either stared, gap-toothed, back at me, the essential information having been wrenched off, or pointed to places that I did not wish to visit.

The day was pleasant, and I was not on a tight schedule, so I was happy to tour the countryside in roughly the right direction until I found a place that I recognised. Presently this happened, but I was heading the wrong way, and not a place beckoned me for turning around.

Patience being a virtue often rewarded – not like some other virtues, which are thankless attributes – I eventually found the entrance to a drive, wide and welcoming, with fields and forestry behind. No doubt there was a farmhouse hidden at the top, but I did not need that, just a few feet to back around and be gone again. And as I slid the vehicle gently around the bend, I saw – a roebuck. A handsome fellow, quite young, in his bright rust summer coat. He was grazing intently by the side of the drive, on some lush grass that had been carefully mown. Cutting alters the structure of grass, so that mown grass is sweeter, a fact of which he was taking full advantage. I should have liked to have seen him closer.

But then, there was not anything stopping me seeing him closer. I switched off the engine, expecting him to look up at least, but he carried on feeding. Dressed in my smart clothes and shiny shoes – I was returning from a funeral – I began to walk up the drive. Not a lively walk, you understand, but the kind of walk you do when you want to get close to a wild animal.

Not everyone's eyes are like ours, and herbivore eyes see very well to either side and behind, with a small blind spot at the front and a similar one directly behind. Approaching deer from the front is quite easy, as long as the wind is the right way.

Periodically, he would lift his head and look around, as a good prey species should, and then return to his grazing. To him, I must have appeared as a small tree.

Continuing to look like a small tree, I walked closer, swaying gently with each footfall, to set my feet squarely on the ground. A stumble or wriggle would not advance my cause.

Then I realised that I had my spectacles in my hand, and that they would be a lot more use on my face, so I brought my hand up in a series of small movements, just the way a branch would sway, and put on my glasses. Yes, he looked even more handsome in focus. If the sunlight caught the glass and reflected in a sudden flash, he might be alarmed, but it was worth the risk. He lifted his head and stared at me quite hard this time. Never make eye contact with an animal if you do not want it to know you are there.

The other important thing to do when stalking is to empty your mind of predatory thoughts. Animals are strongly telepathic, and can tell. With my eyes unthreatening and my mind in that state of suspended awareness that hunters know well, he could pick nothing up from me – except that I was getting closer. How quickly that tree is growing, he may have thought. But then, how sweet this grass is. And he carried on eating.

Goodness knows just how near I might have been able to get to him. On a bright day with absolutely no cover, I was now close enough to see the flies on his face. Surely he could scent me by now? I could admire the different colours of his pelage, the fluffy lined ears, his clean, strong limbs and small shiny hooves. Such a lot of deer on such little feet. Not too much closer and I would be able to smell him.

But still he grazed, and the sun shone on both of us. What a very careless deer. Of course, if I had been stalking to shoot him, I would have had the problem of a big heavy rifle to set up, and he might have noticed that, but as things stood, I was going to be able to tap him on the shoulder soon.

Had I been a predator, he would have been in something of a pickle.

Each time he raised his head, I froze: each time he lowered it and grazed again, I moved a pace or two forwards. Surely I did not still look like a tree?

Well, I wasn't stalking him for my dinner or I might not have become so careless. True I had been walking up to this fellow for more than ten minutes, and covered upwards of a hundred yards in that time, but it was only to see if I could. I moved as he raised his head, and the expression on his face said it all – he had nearly sold his life for a bellyful of sweet grass.

Roe deer are not known for keeping a cool head in a crisis, and he lost his nerve completely. He jumped up, jumped sideways, then to the other side, nearly fell over, rearranged his feet and then took off across the field to the forestry, leaping high into the air every few strides, running zigzag as a deer should. The leaps and swerves are instinctive, to throw a predator off before it can get a grip or measure a pounce.

I remember once meeting a roe running towards me that had been disturbed by some ramblers, and which leaped and swerved so dramatically that it lost its footing and fell in a heap at my feet.

Ah well, I hoped that this young buck had learned something from our encounter, namely not to be so keen on filling his belly that he forgot basic safety rules.

The walk back to the vehicle was accomplished much faster than the walk out, but was not half so much fun. Still, now I knew my way, I could look forward to the drive home.

VII

Ron the spider has been in situ since that warm spell we had in February, which makes me fairly sure he is a male spider, for we have had no eggs, young, or devoured suitors in that time. What I am not so sure about is if he is a native specimen. Though Ron himself is small, unassuming and dull in colour, his web, taking up much of one of the dining-room windows, is rather unusual both in design and strength. Whereas a bluebottle that wanders into a normal spiderweb will back out with a lot of buzzing, and leave behind a day of mending for the spider involved, once a bluebottle strays into Ron's web, it is caught. Despite the amount of prey that Ron has accounted for in his time at the window, he grows no larger, so maybe a high degree of nutrition goes straight into web maintenance. Though such a vast construction does not add to the aesthetics of the window, or indeed the dining room, Ron is doing such an excellent job that we have all agreed he can stay. Moreover, he is the soul of discretion. He stays in the window-frame and is never to be seen strolling among the condiments or rifling through the piles of paper that accumulate at one side of the table, it being the sort of place convenient for paper farming. Ingrid, last year's spider, was not so discreet, and gave many an unwary breakfaster a shock as she perambulated across the tablecloth, all hairy legs and armpits, pausing to tap her forelegs against the crockery. Ingrid was definitely a female spider, though perhaps no lady, for she ingested several suitors before producing a cocoon full of young. This could be a panicky discovery for arachnaphobes, but is nothing new in our household, where reasonable behaviour is tolerated. The baby spiders seemed all over the window for a day or two, while the strong ones hunted down and ate their weaker brethren, and the hens picked at some of the more adventurous, though telling us that big spiders tasted bitter and tiny ones were barely worth the pecking. It is at times like these that one hesitates to shoo hens out of the house, for they are at least doing something helpful, and we seldom see woodlice indoors now. Anyway, Ingrid's mortal remains were found in a corner one day, she having fulfilled her biological legacy, and all the evidence of her existence was at last cleaned away. We are most reluctant to harm spiders, for they do so much good, but the side-effect is cobwebs, which do not seem to be much in fashion right now. I would like to think that some of the more pretentious interior design magazines might take this matter up, perhaps exploring the delights of spiderwebs sprayed silver and gold for Christmas, once the spiders had finished with them.

Meanwhile, Ron, or maybe with a web shaped like that we should be calling him Bruce, occupies a part of the window we don't use much anyway, and keeps the flies in check. Early in the morning, as the first cup of tea is steaming gently before me, he will sit just inside the lowest corner of his web and watch me with some of his eyes. The web at daybreak is at its best, for Ron will have mended any tears caused by the previous day's quarry. I have other eyes watching me as well, for once I stand up to return my mug to the kitchen, at least one dog, and this morning it is two, will be asking to come on my rounds with me. I have a lot of traps to check right now, and just as Ron has to keep his web in good order, so I have to empty and re-set my traps, maybe putting more or different bait in, maybe siting the traps in different places according to where I have seen tell-tale signs of where my quarry runs. I cannot see scent, but my dogs can follow it, and by watching where they go, I can often find better places to lay my traps. What Ron does by instinct, I do by intellect. Everyone's life is someone else's dinner, whether vertebrate or invertebrate, and we near the top of the food chain will one day provide sustenance to those at the very bottom of it. There is a completeness about this. Though we lead vastly different lives, Ron and I both dance to Nature's orchestra, each living in the corner of our particular window.

VIII

My road took me past Jim's old forge. Not the forge he used at the height of his career, you understand, but the much smaller red-brick building to which he moved his workshop when he began to scale down his commitments prior to retirement. Jim was both a farrier and a blacksmith, working with iron and fire to make and fit every kind of shoe to every kind of horse, or, if he liked you and the mood took him, everything from elaborate wrought-iron decorative wear to utilitarian farm tools. Anything made by him fitted to the hairsbreadth, balancing in the hand, at the hinge or on the hoof exactly as it should.

Horse owners grew anxious when Jim announced his retirement plans, which were as meticulous as his shoeing. The shoe for the work was Jim's bread and butter, but where he showed his real skill was in remedial shoeing. Jim could fit corrective metal to a horse's foot to counterbalance any mistake of Nature, so that a foal's legs, crooked at birth, would straighten as it grew, so that an older horse, rough in its gait for this reason or that, would move more sweetly. If the foot was right, the strain would be reduced on back, legs and joints, and the horse would benefit hugely as indeed would those who rode it. Was the foot weak and crumbling? Were the feet odd in shape, or not paired, was there old injury or the tell-tale signs of disease or hardship in the past? Jim could hammer out a shoe from a strip of steel that would make the best of the bad job before him. Was the horse an awkward cuss, that would lean and fidget? Jim never lost his patience. Was it dangerous? Like all farriers, he had his share of horse-induced injuries, but for the most part a combination of genuine rapport and acute observation protected him from horses' worst excesses. I remember him telling me about a horse with a reputation for savage biting. "I gave 'un a piece of treacle toffee" he chuckled, miming the jaw-work of a horse so occupied. "'E couldn' bite me then!"

Racehorses were a particular love of his. Many were the horses whose futures were saved by Jim being in the right place at the right time. If a horse broke down on the track, Jim would have a wedge under its heel straight away, immediately lifting the strain on the damaged tendon and enabling the horse to travel home or to the veterinary surgery without further mishap. A horse in a lorry will be changing its weight from foot to foot to balance itself, and the difference between the supported and unsupported injury could be critical. That wedge of Jim's was better than any amount of strapping, and he usually had a couple in his pocket. Of course, the horse would be bandaged as well, but it was the wedge that gave that vital extra stability.

Racehorse feet can be tricky as well, often not as strong as those of other breeds, and with the constant change from racing plates to exercise shoes and back again presenting its own challenges. Jim was a past master at fitting a shoe onto the less-than-perfect foot, and he was very proud of having shod a Grand National winner, not just for the race but for all of its retirement as well.

Once a photographer had asked to take pictures of Jim at work in his forge, and those photographs were outstanding. I can see them now in my mind's eye: the steam, the river of molten metal, the arcing of the sparks as he shaped the shoe on his anvil, his own face, lined and reamed from years of such work, with sweat dripping down.

While Jim's craftsmanship was in no doubt, few people knew the depth of knowledge that he had. Because I was interested, he loaned me some old books of his on corrective farriery, and they were absolutely fascinating. He had not remained within the boundaries of those books but expanded and built upon their foundations to a formidable range of expertise. Most importantly, Jim knew horses. Where many modern farriers never ride a horse, Jim had grown up in a different time, and he understood shoeing both from the ground and on the horse. He loved a shoeing challenge but appreciated a well-behaved horse with unremarkable feet as well. You could learn a lot from Jim as he drank his tea and smoked a roll-up between horses. Slow-spoken and utterly Sussex, he had a twinkle in his eye and a grand sense of humour.

It was impossible to drive past the old forge without a pang. Jim never got to enjoy his retirement: in fact, he never managed to retire. His funeral was family only, to the great sadness of his many friends, and I hope those wonderful books and the photographs of which he was so proud were appreciated by his distant relatives, for Jim had never married. I was surprised the old forge was still there, having imagined it long since turned into housing, for it is five, maybe six years since the lurking illness claimed him.

Weeds curl around the door, but not around my memories. I can still smell the tobacco, hear his deep chuckle, those things that preceded another tale or a juicy piece of gossip. There are and will be other farriers with his knack and talents, though not with his background or beginnings. Jim, it was a privilege to know you, and you are sorely missed.

IX

The lane carries more horse traffic than vehicular, so it was safe to stop when I saw the heap in the road. Heaps that move might require assistance. This one consisted of a kestrel that looked up peevishly, thought about taking us on, decided perhaps not, and took to the air, carrying something. As it did so, a very small rodent ran across the lane into the grass verge so fast that it was a blur, and another tiny rodent remained dead in the middle of the road. What was the story behind that? Before I could get out and confirm any identities, two vehicles materialised behind me, probably the only two to use this route for the next few hours, and as I was blocking the road much as the small falcon had been, I drove on.

Several miles further on, another wildlife drama had taken place. This time, there lay a stoat and a rabbit freshly dead by the side of the road. Had they both been hit while taking part in their own life-or-death struggle? Had the rabbit been run over and the stoat paused, fatally, to sniff it? We would never know.

I opened the big gate, and drove through. Now we were on tracks that were normally impassable, but the dry summer has made them drivable. A strong scent of crushed water mint followed our progress, and dragonflies swooped all around us. We parked at the top of the slope, in the heather, and walked on down to the water. A host of mallard sprang to the 'clump' of the vehicle door shutting, and starburst into the sky, leaving ripples and a few feathers in their wake. The water level was low despite recent heavy showers. Like the track, it would take a lot of rain to bring back to normal. Well, it was helpful not to have to walk so far. The dog, delighted at a change of scene, pottered about in the shallows as my colleague scattered barley. 'Feeding the pond' we called it, but it was the ducks that were being fed. Even as we were there, small flights of mallard veered over the top of us, singing the wind through their wings, impatient for us to leave so that they could eat. Often the teal would come as well. It is a magical place at any time of year, but especially now with autumn on the way. Gnats sang above my head, and dragonflies flew so close in pursuit that I could feel the draught from their dry-paper rattle of wings. Scents were layered heavily in the still air, the rankness of the bracken competing with the honeyed sweetness of the thistle heads and the heather, water mint lingering at every footfall.

A handful of times each year, the tranquillity of the pond would be disturbed for an hour or two as the flying duck were harvested. The start of the season was nearly upon us again, and we were restive with it. There would be the excitement of the winnowing wings approaching, the duck calls, a cacophony of shots and splashes, then the waiting dogs sent to power through water that would now be deep and chill. Each of us would take home the foundations of delicious meals, and the pond would sleep again until the next time. Skimming the surface, taking what the population could comfortably give us, that is the hunters' way. Nothing too much, never too often. Meanwhile, a host of wildlife enjoyed the seclusion and security of the hidden water. We made ready to depart, and the dragonflies rattled and skimmed in our wake.

X

All hands on deck before daybreak, for today the pheasant poults are coming. The idea is to have them in their pens at first light, for then they have the whole day in which to settle, and a day is a long time when you are only seven weeks old. Also the journey is cooler for them at night, packed for their own safety in crates. So many per crate, so many per pen, so how many crates is that, young Tom? Young Tom, enjoying a baptism of fire in his school holidays by being allowed to help the gamekeeper, never considered that maths would be part of the job. Maths is very much part of the job if it is done properly: how many feed hoppers per pen, how many drinkers, all cleaned and disinfected, how many pens for how many pheasants? The pens are huge, erected around natural woodland, like living wild but safer. Once the poults are well enough grown, they will live properly wild in the woods, but they need more protection at this stage. How much disinfectant, how many sacks of food per week? You cannot afford to run out, and there is only so much space to store.

The pens have been well prepared. It is not just a matter of fencing in a suitably large area of woodland, but a great deal of pest control. The strip of electrified fence running around the perimeter to dissuade vermin at ground level, the wire surrounds, the glittering discs and flapping white pieces of plastic hung on high to repel avian predators, will only do so much good. There is nothing else you can do about birds of prey, which are protected, except hope that most of them will dislike the fluttering and flashing objects around the pen, and go and seek their dinner elsewhere. A few poults will be taken, during which time it is to be hoped that the others will learn to hide in the ample cover as soon as they see that dread silhouette. We work strictly within the law at every level, which means that we have to set snares for the foxes as we can no longer use the dogs*. This snare here had a vixen in it the first night it was set. Not only do we need fox wires around the perimeter of the pen, we are wise to set them on nearby rides that lead to it as well. We have been in the habit of running a good dog through the inside of the pen, to make sure that nothing nasty has taken up residence despite all these precautions, but of course nowadays we have to have a gun handy in case the dog flushes a fox. Foxes will get into the pens no matter what, and a dog is by far the best way of finding them: you do not want to be releasing your precious poults into a pen that has a fox waiting, for it will kill the lot in one go.

Grey squirrels are a problem too. We all know how they kill trees and young songbirds, but they are a menace in other ways. See here where they have chewed through the pipes that feed the drinkers? We wage constant war against the squirrels, and Tom would earn a fair bit of pocket-money if the bounty were re-introduced, for he has become quite the lad at trapping them.

The vehicle from the game farmer arrives, towing the trailer loaded with crates, and after a brief pause for introductions and discussion of where we would all be going and in what order, he sets off after the 'keeper. It is an interesting drive in parts, but at least the dry year means that we can get down the rides without being suddenly becalmed in a deep muddy rut. The branches scrape off the roof and sides here and there, and we jolt to a standstill by the first pen. How many crates, Tom?

Opening the first crate, the gamekeeper scrutinises his poults very carefully. These seem good: bright of eye, well-grown and lively. They always are good from this source, but nothing is taken for granted. He

*This was written after the Hunting ban

nods briefly, says "These'll do" to the delivery driver, who accepts the understated compliment with an inner smile of relief while the young birds scurry away into the cover. Presently they will venture out to eat and drink, and show the way to the ones that are shy of or unaccustomed to the feeders. Tom is now struggling round the pen with a sack of feed, emptying small amounts at frequent intervals for the poults to find.

For the gamekeeper, the real work starts in earnest now. For Tom, a steep learning curve coupled with a greater tiredness and more job satisfaction than school has ever given him. For the delivery driver, who also works on the game farm, a long journey back and then comprehensive disinfection of vehicle, crates and outer clothing. Tomorrow will start three hours before dawn for him, delivering another load of poults to another gamekeeper, seeing them approved and then released safely 'to wood' at the break of day.

XI

He was a most beautiful creature, in the way that only those bred for a purpose can be. His plumage, ruffled from the long journey, glittered in the weak sunlight, and I could see that his emergency travelling accommodation had cost him the neatness of his tail feathers, for instead of a proud waterfall of iridescence, they were tattered and spiked. Yet he took the eye with his symmetry, in the way that a racehorse or a greyhound does. His profile was a series of proud curves, his legs bestrode the ground like those of a tiny Colossus. He had missed death by a whisker. He was a gamecock.

He had come to me as a staging post on his route to safety, travelling first across the water, then along England's spine, south until he could go south no further, and whither he was bound I will tell no-one. Bred in the purple, pedigreed like a Thoroughbred horse, he was far too valuable to betray, far too desirable to the wrong people. I should have loved to have kept him. This was, thankfully, out of the question too decisively to even provide more than a flutter of temptation. I was welcome to keep him, to dance attendance on my cosy everyday hens and brighten my days with his arrogant good looks, but he would attract too much interest, and the wrong sort. Like a jewel too rare and precious, he could never, for his own safety, be displayed. Furthermore, he would give himself away, as he now proved, by stretching his wings and crowing. He was pleased to be out of his carrying crate, and did not know that in a few hours, he would be travelling on.

I gave him food and water, and he proved himself not only mortal, but a typical fowl, by knocking over the one and messing in the other. Twice I replaced with clean, and twice he scattered and soiled his rations. I left him to settle, for he needed this respite, and he crowed again and again, it being in his nature to seek out rivals, and having found them, to destroy them, or else himself in the process. Gentle with people, he had been bred and born with an implacable hatred of the males of his own kind. He was a responsibility that I did not want, but I had not been able to turn my back on him in his hour of need.

My homely old hens gathered to speak to him with their soft, interrogative clucks and skirls, hoping that the handsome young man was here to stay, and why had I not let him out? He spoke quietly back, more at home now, and I marvelled at his strength and the exquisite sculpture of his body. Though only a young bird, his legs were sturdy, and already bore substantial spurs, and his comb had been tonsured close to his head. Even those kept for ornamental purposes, as he would now be, would sometimes need the latter treatment, to prevent mutilation by another of his kind. You can take the cock out of the main, but you can never take the main out of the cock. He was not, as my Irish friends would have it, 'for eejits'. He was not for me, either, much as I would have liked it to be so.

I made some telephone calls, and then he was back in his crate, though not without quite a struggle. Did he but care, he had far more space in there than battery hens in a cage or broilers in a dark shed, and it was only for a few more hours now. He had had enough of travelling and complained bitterly, but quietened once I put a blanket over his transport and started the engine. He had certainly been well looked after. I dropped him off at dusk, and he had two more staging posts to go.

The telephone call came the next day, through an intermediary, because I had not wanted to know the whereabouts of his final destination. His new owner had recognised at once the ruffled rarity that had stepped out of the crate for the last time and into a quarantine run, where he could hear and see other fowl but not mix with them. Once he had proved himself healthy, these birds would be his wives, but having seen him, his saviour vowed to obtain some hens of the same breeding. Those bloodlines were too precious to lose. The cruel pastime for which he had been bred, and which has rightly been outlawed here for upwards of one hundred and fifty years, has made such as he almost extinct. It is true that many different types of gamefowl still exist and are exhibited at poultry shows all over the country, but those are not in the same league, not by a long way. Once you set eyes on the real thing, you know beyond doubt that you are looking at pure quality.

So he will live in obscurity, but he will be happily free-range, surrounded by his hens, and he will get the chance to pass on his royal genes. As for me, I was glad enough to have been a link in the chain of his salvation, and pleased to hear that his new owner was not only delighted with him, but appreciated truly what he now owned.

Then came the most wonderful surprise: would I like a brace of pullets from his breeding this year? The hens are dull in plumage, but still of that athletic build, and layers of long, pointed white eggs. Being female, they would attract no interest, and of course they would not crow. Only I would know of the flawless bloodlines behind them.

I think you can guess the answer.

XII

All the ingredients for a splendid wedding were present. There was a beautiful bride and a dashing groom; most unusually, there was also a cast of extremely well-behaved, polite children. Guests were many and varied: a collection of Formidable Aunts and Genial Uncles, some local farmers, and plenty of fieldsports afiçionados emerging immaculate from muddy vehicles more used to carrying fierce terriers, fishing equipment and empty cartridges. Guests came from afar, too, having paid the happy couple the compliment of travelling from the more inaccessible corners of these islands, and even from the Colonies. Mothers-in-law were each delightful people, welcoming and warm. The Matron of Honour was a bitch, but an exquisitely beautiful one, with a silky coat and plumed tail, and she wore her ribbons and bows with dignity. Me, I had shaken the moths out of my best suit, checked the pockets for mice, and definitely emerged from the filthiest vehicle, but in considerably smarter order than usual (several people commented on this). The bride arrived in an elderly but spotless and beribboned Range Rover.

The Service is a private matter, so I will simply say that it was in keeping with this special day, as was the reception, which latter was held at a lovely old farmhouse. We were all in a pleasantly relaxed state when two things happened: the Matron of Honour, now free from her ceremonial trappings, came to me and indicated with a sweep of her tail and a glowing look from her huge brown eyes, that it was dusk and therefore time to go on patrol, and a cry of alarm from one of the guests alerted us to the fact that one of the more unusual wedding presents had escaped. There was a screeching of chairs being pushed back as the local hunters and shooters rose to the occasion, and a particularly feral old biddy took off her diamond earrings and slipped them into her pocket. A copper horn with much history was lifted from the wall, and The Hunt was on!

Gerald, who always carried a hound-eared copy of the Hunting Ban in his pocket, was fervently flicking through the pages to see how we could recapture this beast and remain within the law. We had one hound to flush it out with – we were allowed another. The White Witch disappeared into the lee of a hedge and presently reappeared with the shade of a useful and much-loved hound, part terrier, part border collie, part angel, and the Lady Master lieu'd him in – go, Henry! We needed a gun – who had the nearest gun? One of the neighbours made a telephone call and the gun was on its way with all paperwork in order. Only thing was, the wedding present was one-half of a breeding pair, and we didn't want it shot. Luckily, I had my longnet in the vehicle from the last time I'd been ferreting, so I started to run it out across the field in what I hoped would be the right place. The Hunt Secretary, with enormous presence of mind, took a cap from all the guests, and the local gamekeeper took photographs as well as charge of the beating line. It was important to have the photographs in case out-of-work saboteurs appeared and claimed that we were hunting illegally. Gerald had reached the part in his notes that confirmed that we could use the two dogs to flush the mammal for research and study purposes as well as to recapture it, so long as certain criteria were fulfilled. As the scientific wildlife researcher on the premises, I covered part of that, we needed to recapture the quarry and re-unite it with its mate, we had the landowner's permission, and we just had to establish whether the quarry could be classified as a wild mammal. The Aunt who had brought them confirmed that he could be a 'fiery wee rascal' and that was wild enough for our purposes.

The bride was not going to miss out on any of this, so she hitched up her skirts and, collecting the smallest bridesmaid, kicked off her shoes and skimmed across the fields like a swallow. The groom and best man, always working as a team, formed a flank with the bride's brother, who nobly whipped off his gold brocade waistcoat to use as a flag if the quarry needed turning. The remaining bridesmaids comforted its mate, which was becoming distressed at the loss of her partner, and emitting a high-pitched keening. Not being experienced with this type of animal (it is normally only seen in the northernmost areas) we hoped that it might respond to this. The Aunt confirmed that they are much more settled when paired up, and as we would like to form a breeding colony of these charming creatures, this was good news.

Henry Hound and the Huntsman drew steadily down the hedge, and finally we heard a 'Tally-ho!' from Joe at the corner as the quarry broke cover. The Matron of Honour gathered herself and sprinted across the field in its wake, the gold brocade waistcoat flashed in the dying sunset to turn it towards my longnet, but it headed for the bride who, displaying far too much of her long, elegant legs, flapped her skirts at it and turned it again. It headed for one of the county's best netball players, who almost had it, but it feinted and dodged round her, straight into the jaws of Henry Hound. He retrieved the creature with some difficulty to the Huntsman. "Careful!" bellowed the Aunt, "Let me take him".

The Formidable Aunt gathered the escapee, which was spitting and hissing and gnashing surprisingly big teeth. Clearly a specialist, she took it and soothed it into a state of calmness without being bitten while we, wise in the ways of animals, kept back to avoid stressing the little fellow any further. The bridesmaids approached shyly, hoping to be allowed to stroke it, and the gamekeeper took its photograph to prove that we had captured it without injury. Henry Hound paused, wagged, licked a few hands, grinned in that way he used to, and then evaporated into the darkness from whence he had come. The Aunt signalled for the quivering, keening little animal in the carrying-box to be brought forward and reunited with her mate.

"Now then, you naughty wee haggis" she said.

XIII

Big-boned full-bodied hounds, not in a hurry, not dallying, drawing steadily up the Adur. We followed in shirt-sleeve order, some of us hatted against the sun. By the river was a little eddy of breeze, but nothing much. Tall comfrey, hairy-leaved, nodded as the pack searched for a whiff of mink, parting the reeds, questing the roots and rocks for their quarry. "Try over," called the huntsman, and obedient hounds swam the short distance across the water, to shoulder through the vegetation on the far side.

We walked the riverside path that was fissured from the long dry spell. In one of the fields, hay was curing: if you lifted it, it was still green and sappy underneath. Such an elusive quarry we sought, such a damaging one, an animal from which bird nor fish nor small mammal could hide. One of the hounds chimed once, twice, and the others came up to check. Up on the bridge, one of the followers was signalling that the mink had just passed him. Within seconds, the pack was spilling in its wake. Not for long, for the mink had hidden in a pile of rocks further up from the bridge, and hounds were marking enthusiastically where it had gone in. One of the more canny hounds, closely watched by the whipper-in, was marking further along, indicating that the mink had not stayed in his rock pile, but travelled on downstream. This was endorsed by one of the terriers.

As the unravelling scent told its story, we watched the pack carefully following the mink's trail, pausing to confirm here and there where the scent varied in its intensity. Such intricate hound work: such a pleasure to watch.

Information seemed to peter out in the roots of a tree and, knowing that trick, hounds and followers looked up into the branches, lest our mink had gone upwards. But no, it was fortressed in a tunnel under the roots. Often they will depart again, when they judge it politic to do so, and to aid this decision, the pack was taken away to explore a small stream leading off the main waterway. One discreet observer remained behind.

Meanwhile, we tackled a flimsy bridge, some stock fencing, not too arduous, and some friendly sheep, and watched hounds pushing their resolute way downstream. Damselflies and dragonflies darted around us, the latter including some huge striped fellows, the wide-bodied jets of the riverside. While hounds searched for mink scent, human nostrils were treated to the freshness of crushed water-mint, the honeyed sweetness of thistle flowers and, by way of balance, that green pondy smell of stirred-up river and wet hound.

We found nothing along there, but as we returned along the bank, a holloa told us what we had been hoping to find: our mink had left his tree-roots and was away!

Even human nostrils could detect the scent of peevish mink at the point of his departure, and an exciting hunt followed. The mink made good his escape despite some diligent hound work, but that is hunting. There was plenty more river left to draw, but I had to leave at that point and get back to work.

I had thoroughly enjoyed watching hounds doing what hounds do best, and seeing the unobtrusive teamwork of the hunt staff. Hounds in the water and hustling along the river banks, heads down, sterns waving, followers keeping pace on the banks without interfering, everyone relaxed but alert, searching for signs of the elusive mink.

That was my last view of them as they rounded the loop in the river, and I set off across the fields for home. I would be out with them again as soon as ever I could.

XIV

The hungry combines stand still in the farmyard as I pass. The sun is not yet up to dry the dew, and the morning is still rubbing its eyes. The dogs and I negotiate the padlocked gates each in a way that suits us, and start the walk along the track. Pigeons rise from the stubbles and flap heavily down again, sated. In the wildflower meadow, a single skylark is singing at full throttle, an amazing amount of noise to come out of such a small bird, and beautiful to hear withal. A pair of English partridge whirrs out of the long grass ahead, and breaks to left and right like fighter aircraft. Such a pity they did not raise their brood. What became of them? Impossible to say, for there are so many hungry maws here to feast on young partridges, from the foxes and badgers, through the hedgehogs, mink, squirrels and stoats (not forgetting the rats of course) to the avian predators, the crows, magpies, herons and raptors. Most years we have a partridge family, and we who walk the farm are delighted to see them, and wish them no harm. This year, I shall miss the little covey that often brightens my day during a winter walk.

The dogs, as ever, are scouring the ground for scent, and then the horizon for movement. There is not a great deal that escapes their notice. Rabbits hop into cover in a leisurely fashion, too far ahead and too close to refuge to make it worth the dogs' while to run after them. Wise dogs learn early not to squander their energy chasing the impossible. I send them to the hedge with a gesture – the morning is too pure to sully with speech – and they bore blissfully along the bottom of it, seeking the hidden rabbits within. The tops of the hedges are thatched with mauve blackberry flowers: we should have a bumper crop this year. Sometimes a very dry year encourages fruiting in the wild vegetation, because it is programmed for the survival of the species in a way that domestic strains have had subdued in them. Our apple tree at home, for instance, is casting its tiny fruits for lack of water, but the blackberry is determined to pass its genes on. So, unfortunately, is the ragwort, and I bend to pull a stem that has escaped the farmer's purge on it.

A rattle of paws on stubble alerts me to the first good chase of the day, where the dogs have flushed a rabbit from the hedge. One dog is extracting himself from the tangled bramble and briar that the rabbit thought it could hide in, and the other is swerving about in a gathering cloud of dust and bits of straw, spinning the rabbit into confusion as it races for the far hedge. The rabbit gets there a snap ahead of the dog, which latter returns to me, eyes sparkling, tongue lolling, and a big happy grin on her face. The ground is too hard to run dogs in earnest, but a sprint here and there keeps them cheerful. Just as I am thinking that the meadowsweet and scabious combination footing this hedge is one of the best I have seen, the smaller dog catches a rabbit that sat a fraction too long in the long grass, and presents it to me. His face is garlanded with goosegrass, and numerous sticky green seed-pods are tangled in his coat. Very fetching. He is far too busy to linger, and is off again to find another rabbit, or possibly a rat, in the ditch.

Ahead and to the right, a roe doe with a well-grown youngster steps into the road that right-angles our track. She glides into the cover on the far side, but the fawn is curious, and lingers to look at us, huge ears framing its delicate face. The dogs put invisible leads on themselves and come to heel. The doe tries to get her child to follow, but it won't, for it is far too interested in us. Quite a few minutes of maternal concern pass by before a very foolish young deer eventually follows its mother, who presumably gives it a good telling-off.

Our way takes us back towards the yard, where the combines have coughed into life. Soon the stately procession will sail into the fields to continue reaping our daily bread. Already it is getting too hot for dogs, and they pause to refresh themselves from the horse trough, while the ponies lay their ears back and complain about the intrusion of greasy carnivore snouts in their nice clean water. Breakfast calls, and we head back home, me to begin the day and the dogs to sleep through it. Very sensible, if you ask me.

XV

Very early on a summer morning is a good time to be out. The old grey dog thought so too, running ahead of me in the heavy dew, then bounding back for a wag and a lick to tell me what fun this all is, before scooting around the field in springing strides, as only a longdog can. She has me to herself this morning: all dogs need one-to-one time with their owners, and she was loving every moment.

We take the footpath past the demurely cudding sheep, then over the stile into the wheat. She can't leap the way she used to, so she flattens under the stile as I climb over it, to be nicely underfoot as I step back onto the ground. It is an old joke between us.

In the wheat, she is all business, a dog who knows her trade to the inch. Once a poacher's dog, now a moucher's dog, and one of my dearest friends these many years. She would like to hunt the tramlines that cut through the crop, and fixes her huge eyes on me, asking.

I know this farmer and he does not mind, so I send her on with a gesture and she disappears from sight. The crop is not yet at the stage where she might damage it, and, unlike barley, oats or bearded wheat, it has no sharp whiskers to damage her. There is a rushing, and out comes a fleeing rabbit.

Hunting by scent, her eyes, ears and nose full of water from the dew, she comes snorting out after it, then recognises a lost cause and plunges back in to find another one. Sometimes I see her head appear, sometimes a disembodied tail, then two-thirds of the dog rises above the greenery in a porpoise leap, and she is running hard. Straight up the tramline in front of her is a half-grown rabbit that is evidently off his territory. On a straight run, this old dog could not match any but an equally old rabbit, but she makes up in wits what she has lost in speed and, as the rabbit turns, she sidesteps accurately and lifts him off the ground.

Black with wetness now, she lies down to get her breath back, while I sit beside her, listening to skylarks. Presently, she gets to her feet, nudges me with her long nose, and I get up too, a lot less gracefully than she. I go over the gate at the hinge end, she slides under the barbed wire, and now we are in the set-aside. I cast her off like a falcon, and she quarters the ground like the expert she is, moving at that deceptive all-day trot, not so fast that she will miss anything, not so slow as it looks. Here and there, a rabbit skitters away, birds fly up, she hunts on, her whole being a thrill of scent. Ahead of her, from a clump of grass that you would have thought could barely shelter a vole, a roe doe erupts. "Leave it!" I shout, though she knows not to chase.

She gives me a wave of her tail in acknowledgement, and plunges her nose back into the rich scent on the ground, while the roe bounds across the field into the woods, all russet coat and flashing white rump. Three pigeons fly over, and I am cursed by crows.

The next field has cattle in it, and I don't cross cattle fields with a dog if I can help it, so I skirt the woods, cut across the corner, and after an undignified scramble over the ditch which had fewer brambles the last time I did this, I am at the bottom end of the sheep field.

This is quite far enough for an old dog, and although she is moving as freely as a youngster now, she will be stiff later if she does much more. There is a lovely smell by the hedge, to which she adds her own liquid comment, and then she canters after me, evading the attentions of a curious lamb with a neat sideways skip.

She sniffs blissfully at the rabbit in my pocket, which I shall cook for her supper, and then falls into step behind me. I turn to unlatch the last gate, she follows me through it, and I gently pull one of her silken ears.

Her coat is wet and spiky, her eyes are shining with happiness, her great jaw open in a huge grin. How to make an old lady happy. What precious hours these are, hunting together, man and dog, for hundreds of thousands of years.

XVI

Learning to stay completely still and quiet is a prerequisite for anyone who wants to learn the ways of the wild things, as is the ability to keep an open and enquiring mind, for every time you go out, you will learn something new. Thus a simple stroll with the dogs on a drowsy summer morning becomes the pleasantest of educations. We were out before the heat began to sting, the dew still thickly silvering the grass, a luscious scent of vanilla and honey coming from the hedge where wild rose, honeysuckle and elder blossom entwined.

Elder blossom is intriguing: at a short distance, it has an acrid, civet smell overlaying out its sweetness, but at point-blank range its scent is intoxicating. Late in the day, these glorious aromas will lie heavily layered in the air, but now they were fresh, new and crisp.

Along the ditch, the dogs exercised a rabbit or two, and then looking across the set-aside, we saw the most charming sight. A fledging of baby skylarks was learning to hover, three, four, five feet above the grass seedheads, and then plop! back down again. "How can you do this and sing?" we could almost hear them thinking.

Five little brown burrs rose and fell on their new wings; further across, you could see another skylark kindergarten engaged in the same task. They have so many foes, these little things that nest on the ground. Crows, magpies, jays, foxes, hedgehogs, cats, stoats, badgers and more yet, though the lack of human traffic on the footpath had been a plus for them this year due to the foot and mouth restrictions.

Then one young skylark rose so close to me that I could have reached out and touched it. It was hovering really well and had not considered me at all, nor the dogs standing like statues beside me, steadied by no more than a thought and an outstretched finger. Low and fast like a fighter aircraft came a parent skylark across the grass-tips, and both adult and youngster fell hidden into the greenery. You could imagine the lecture the little fellow would get, once safety had been reached. I relaxed my restricting hand, and the dogs flowed across the landscape once more.

Into the small wood, preceded by scurrying rabbits and the raucous cry of a jay, the farm dog is off with a purpose. Presently a volley of barks confirm that he has found a fox.

Already one of my lurchers has left my side to join him, but she is ten years old. Though her spirit is undiminished, her legs are not what they were. Beside me the very old dog stands, trembling with eagerness, knowing better than to forge after them, but wanting to so very much. The other has not reached the fox in time: a pure, silvery holloa sounds from the farmer at the edge of the wood, then a sharp "Tally-ho back!"

Again, I freeze in my tracks as a strange fox passes me only a dozen feet away, giving me a good look at him. He is dressed for a special occasion: white shirt, white tag on his brush, plenty of white about his body, a smart bachelor-about-town, a stark contrast to most foxes about at this time of year, which look distinctly tattered and careworn from raising their cubs.

The old grey dog is off after him, and my own voice alerts the other two, who appear out of the thick undergrowth and, noses down, follow in his wake. I follow in turn, with difficulty, through to the old earth which was not used this year, hoping that we could mark him to ground.

This is not the resident farm fox, who lives at the other end of the property, but a stranger. Two days before, I saw a different strange fox on the boundary, a long sandy one as opposed to this chunky dandy with the bespoke tailoring.

But he had not gone to ground. He was off across the neighbour's fields, and too far ahead to do business with. The dogs return, panting, and lie in the brook to cool off, the young farm dog then getting hot again by doing several laps of honour round the field. The old girls roll in the grass like puppies, enormously pleased with their hunt even if it had been unsuccessful this time.

The new fox made his presence felt, hanging around the farm buildings and picking off the free-range hens instead of staying up the valley and eating rabbits. It was nearly a week later that he was found in the live-trap, unmistakably the same fellow in his smart suit. So it was that he died a felon's death, shot at dawn, and the hens would be safe until the next one came in.

The skylarks would be safe too for a little while longer, and we hoped that they might even be able to raise a second brood, now that one of their many enemies was out of the way.

XVII

I have spent much of my life involved with Thoroughbred horses, but by the time I met Casey, age and infirmity had joined forces with common sense, and I never had the slightest desire to ride him. Nor had many other people.

He was a big – and I do mean big – beautifully-made mahogany bay horse, with a slight Roman nose, an air of hauteur, and what is nowadays known as 'attitude'. Casey was broken-in late, after several different attempts by different people, and went in and out of racing yards large and prestigious, small and expert, and smaller and prepared to take a gamble, with very little to show for it except a dicky leg and even more attitude. On the way, he decided that all-weather gallops were for mugs, and he didn't like men, dogs or even other horses all that much.

Casey was taken home and given to a girl to ride; as he was nearer eighteen hands than seventeen, even getting a headcollar on him was an act of faith. Certainly, where Casey was concerned, you got further faster with trickery than ever you would with asking nicely or even firmly. What can you do with a highly intelligent horse that can gallop and jump but won't, is of dubious soundness, bucks, rears and spins with a suddenly dropped shoulder, and greets any overtures of friendship with laid-back ears and a sneer? Hasten slowly, says the German proverb, and so she did.

Being a friend of the family, I got to know Casey almost too well. From time to time I was involved in doing odd jobs of care and maintenance for him, when even venturing into the field with him required nerves of steel. That first year, there was a sudden influx of foxes. Casey hated them, and would charge after them, striking out with a lethal foreleg. I never let a dog near him. His education was battle after battle, but in the autumn, he went hunting.

He was an exasperating hunter: cowardly despite his undoubted ability, ungenerous in any of the frequent hunting situations where a horse needs to give that bit extra, dangerous to sit upon and none too pleasant to be near. But, as a failed racehorse who was too blemished to show, not scopey enough to show-jump, too cowardly to event and too bolshie for dressage, hunting was the only career open to him. His young rider persisted, and hunting worked its magic as it does on so many sour and grudging horses. Casey went in one season from pain in the neck to superstar.

Always a gentleman with hounds (which were obviously not dogs) and not caring one way or the other if he was with other horses or on his own, once he got his confidence jumping he became that legendary animal that will go first or last, take his own line, and tackle the most forbidding of obstacles.

Such a big horse, with such a big stride, could cover the ground faster than most, even without his respectable breeding. He would only jump if left alone, would never fiddle a stride or ping off his hocks, but as long as you did things his way, you got there. Still, only the girl would ride him; no stick-insect model type she but a braw country lass, a fine figure in her black and cream, turning more than a few male heads.

Casey hunted in Sussex and hunted in the Shires as well. Three seasons following hounds made such a different horse of him that he went back onto the racecourse, not as a bully and craven, but a powerful mature steeplechaser. Despite this, he reverted rapidly to the Casey of old, wasted potential, screwball temperament. He was brought back home.

Another season's hunting followed, at the end of which he went point-to-pointing, this time with his strong and dauntless lady owner on board. If this were a fairy story, if there really were adequate rewards for hard work, Casey would have won his races, but real life is seldom like that. What he did do was enjoy them, give his young friend ride after ride of excitement, sheer fun, eating the ground with his monstrous stride, kicking the fences behind him, taking off far beyond the wings and landing equally far the other side. Casey was happy.

There are many horses like Casey, but few people with the time, skill or inclination to indulge them. It is almost always hunting that brings them back into the real world, and tames the hooligan in them just enough. Hunting gave Casey a wonderful life, the way no other equine discipline could have done. And a month ago, when Casey injured himself beyond repair while turned out in his paddock, it was hunting that gave him a beautiful and dignified send-off. He was groomed and plaited, and taken to hunt kennels, where a few hounds were let out to spill across the yard, all pied bodies and waving sterns.

Despite the pain in his leg, Casey knew he was going hunting: he arched his neck proudly and pricked his ears. The horn was blown, and he raised his noble head. Casey's last knowledge of life was utter joy.

AUTUMN

I

The great cycles of the year turn as inexorably as the combine blades. Through this memorably hot summer the blossom has drifted, fruits have formed and often shed through lack of water, the grass has grown and been felled first for silage, then for hay. Some have even managed a second cut. Then, remorselessly but without violence, the combines have eaten barley, rape, oats, peas and wheat, with the linseed still waiting. The blades flash and fall in the burning sun, the bales are made and lie, then the shaven stubbles stand forlorn. In many places, the plough turns Sussex clay into furrow almost immediately, but in other places, the stubbles lie, and the wildflowers and selfsown crops show green again. These are the places to find animals and birds making their living.

The warm, clear nights are good for sitting and watching, but today I am here just before daybreak. In the shadows of a bale, another shadow cannot be discerned. Stubble makes for noisy walking, so I get to where

I am going and then sit quietly and comfortably, watching the countryside awaken. If you like watching wildlife, this is a good time to do it. As the sky lightens, pigeons flight to their morning feeding, smaller birds shake off the night and start to cheep and move about, and rodents various scurry amongst the friendly shorn-off stems of what was once a crop. There is plenty to eat for them here. This brings in the predators in turn: the stoat bounces purposefully along, showing off its black tailtip; if there is a weasel, it shows as a bright chestnut flash, an impression on the eye with the animal long gone. Teenage foxes pounce on mice or make unsuccessful dashes after rabbits, or reach up to eat ripe blackberries. They will eat elderberries and sloes, too, the thought of which puts the teeth on edge. Brock is on his way back to bed, having foraged noisily for much of the night. The hedgepig that hoists itself up on legs far too long and skinny for an essentially rotund person, and scuttles past me, was lucky to miss him, for the badger will eat the hedgehog alive, crunching down through quills and bone without a thought. Now here are some rabbits. We shot the fields hard as the combines chewed their way ponderously through the crops, but there are still rabbits, and there will always be rabbits. Young shiny rabbits all smart and dapper, old tattered rabbits with a year of survival behind them, very new rabbits which might or might not reach their first winter, all come out to nibble the new growth. You have to respect weeds for staying so green when all about is parched. The rabbits don't worry: they belong in a climate far more arid than ours, for their origins are in Spain and Portugal. They have many enemies here, but they flourish. In fact, another enemy is approaching them, for myxomatosis has already been seen on this farm, though in the far fields, where it always strikes first. Those rabbits that we shot will have had a quicker end than the myxomatosed ones. Every year the scourge returns, and it is not a happy time except for carrion eaters.

The tabby cat stalks the hedgerow: death in a striped coat. A male by the shape of the head and the burly body, he pads along in search of anything to kill, swinging his head from side to side, to turn the green lamps of his eyes onto whatever little life form he might snuff out. The dog beside me does not move: cats are not on her list. Where the cat will kill anything, no matter how rare or useful, the dog's divisions of wildlife are Get-its and Leave-its, and even Get-its are only pursued at my behest. The cat glows a green glare in the dog's direction, though whether he has actually seen us or not is debatable.

The sun is sufficiently high now to bestow some warmth, and the first flies are stirring and looking for something red-blooded to torment. I hear a steady thrum of hooves in triple beat: a lone horserider is stealing a canter across the stubbles. No harm done by it, though the ground is harder than I would like to canter a horse upon. Girl and horse swish past steadily, loving the early morning; as the horse draws level with me, he pricks his ears and half-shies, but the rider has no idea that I am there. I wait until they are through the gateway before I stand, moving my stiffened limbs gingerly. The dog stretches and yawns elaborately, a courtesy yawn, not a tired one. "Whither now?" she asks.

Now is for retracing our steps along the hedgeline, the dog to cast for scent, me admiring that richness of the hedgerow's bounty that is seen at its best in the early day. The sloes are magnificent: clustered so tightly on the bough that they look more like bunches of grapes, save for that silvery bloom on their skins. What would you call that colour? Definitely on the blue side of purple, while the umbrellas of elderberries stain dark

red, like their stems. These are feeling the lack of water, you can tell. The rosehips are differing shades of orange and coral, some big, some small, and spindleberries split to show orange in the pink shimmer on the dark wood. Spindles were once made from that fine, hard wood, hence the name, though in the West Country they are known as louseberries, being an old treatment for human lice.

The dog interrupts politely by pushing a rabbit against my leg. Please take it so that I can get another one. I take the rabbit, but see at once that its eyes are swollen shut with myxomatosis, though its limp body is fat enough. I wait until the dog is distracted before discreetly leaving the bunny behind for one of the somethings that will be pleased to find it. They will all be like this in a week or two, then. And so the hound and I continue, past the flocks of feeding woodpigeons that beckon a visit before much longer, and towards that most beguiling combination of smells: coffee, toast and bacon.

II

We were sitting, the young Foxglove and I, tucked into a sheltered spot
on the sidehill, looking at a patch of cover that filled a big hollow on the
other side and then spilled out into three long points: two above, one
below. It had been planted as game cover, and then evolved with tactful
care and a minimum of interference into a lovely piece of countryside.
But it was not just a pretty face – it had work to do. So had this youngster,
for a day out with Uncle involves a certain amount of paying attention. As
children seem to need frequent feeding and watering, we were enjoying
cheese and pickle sandwiches and a flask of coffee between us. I waved
my crust at the little wood, skilfully avoiding a dog's nose. Now then, if
you were a huntsman, where would you send in your hounds, where
would you place your people on point duty, where would you want your
whipper-in, and where would you expect the fox to leave?

Bless the child, he has it spot-on. He checks the wind direction with a few blades of grass, puts his hounds in at the bottom corner of the wood, places his whipper-in at the top just below the rise and knows that the fox will likely make for the next piece of cover, and so probably try to trickle out of the low corner where he can hide in a fold of the land. If there are deer in there, they should run downhill, but it is easiest for the horses to go uphill, so he will put the field-master over here, where he has a clear run either across the open or over that post-and-rail to the triangle field, from where he can take the riders around the hill without interfering with hounds. If the fox is bustled out of the higher corner, he will go straight over the brow of the hill, offering a good view to the whipper-in and a hard ride to the field if they want to stay in touch.

Now, you are the shoot captain. Where will you stand your guns, where do you want your beaters, where will you place your stops and which way will the pheasants fly? Confidently he positions his stops, lines out his beaters and sends his pheasants over the trees across to the next wood and over the guns in the valley. Bravo.

Another day and you are coursing. Where are you bringing in the beat, which way will the hares want to run, where is your slipper in his shy, how will you find the best ground for the dogs, and where will you stand the spectators? The lad knows that the dogs must run on the flat or uphill, but the hares will want to run downhill, therefore although you will bring the beat through here, you will need flankers here, here and here. You can use the spectators as flankers here, and the best place for the slipper is forward of there so that the hounds will be sighted as the hare comes past on a slight uphill gradient.

Coming here after pigeons, where will you put your hide? The flightlines are constant, but you need to find them by observation, and pigeons do not fly for no reason, so you need to know whither and why. You tell me that they will roost in the woods and you will need to go there to find, by massed droppings and the odd feather, where they like to sleep. You will look for ivy-clad trees, and conifers. Next you will need to assess which crops they are raiding and where, for there is little food left in the woods this time of year compared to the earlier bounty of beechmast and acorns. So, looking at the stripped skeletons of the rape fields, you will expect them to be flying across here, and if they are, you can tuck yourself into the hedge and ditch here and be nicely under the flightline.

The child can see so much more in a little patch of woodland than many far older ever will, and I am proud of him. The dog has snaffled my crusts – everything comes to he who waits – and we are ready to move. Can you see anything else we can do with that wood? He can.

The man will cut all the trees down and build houses on it if we let him. I am surprised at the boy's perception, and ask him if he can name the man. He wrinkles his nose in thought. He cannot remember the name, but it's the angry man with two 'Jags' and no council tax.

I own myself startled at the perspicacity of one so young.

III

The old hunter has heard the combines and smelt the change in the air: he needs no calendar. His field offers good horse grazing in that it is not lush and rich, which would make him ill, but instead involves steady walking for steady nourishment. He and the brood mares with whom he lives have the option of the trough or the small stream to drink from, there is shelter by the hedge, he is checked over twice daily, and none of it is enough any more. He knows how the year runs.

A horse that can leap the way he can only stays in a field out of politeness. For the last few mornings, he has brought himself in, pottering around the yard, investigating the garden where he has dead-headed the roses (some of which weren't quite ready for this treatment) and nipped the honey-sweet flowers off the thistles. His stable has been left open so that he can put himself in out of the flies if he wants to, but he has been in and turned around and come out again. He wants human company.

We are sitting in the shade and sorting out saddlery that was put away clean and oiled but now needs a little more work if it is to be brought out and used. It is a pleasant job, and one that cannot be hurried if it is to be done well. Here I am, working the glycerine soap into a growing pile of straps, and a deft young friend is assembling these into recognisable tack. From the assorted metalwork on the other side come "bits – usable", "bits - decorative only", and the "do you know what this was used for", the old-fashioned lorinery from before the days of stainless steel, bearing stubborn rust patches despite their careful storage. Modern bits have evolved, too, made of such as copper and sweet iron, thin for a horse with a fleshy tongue and small mouth, thick for one that has more space to accommodate it, long cheeks and short cheeks, this for a horse that evades by lifting its head, that for one which sets its neck against you. Are any of them harsh? A bit is as harsh as the hand that holds the reins, which is why light hands are such a gift in a horseman.

Then there are stirrups. All sorts of changes in these since I was young, and all of them for the better. Some are angled, some are sprung, most have rubber treads, and you can even get basket-fronted ones that the endurance riders use. Girths and saddles are so much kinder than they were years ago, and you hardly ever see saddle marks or girth galls now, which were once so commonplace. Rugs are more comfortable and easier to fasten, but the horses never change.

The old hunter looms in the doorway, ears cocked. What a lot of saddlery, he says - isn't it time you put some on me? Well, last year you would have already been starting your exercise, my lad, but this year is going to be a little different.* Among the leather straps I find a set of coursing slips, beautifully made by a local saddler. I wonder when these will see use again? Dipping the end of the soap bar into my bucket of water, I rub some soap onto a dry sponge and start to work on them, admiring the brass fittings. In my mind I can see the straining greyhounds, one wearing a white collar and the other the red, the slipper breaking into a run as they surge ahead in these very slips, leather supple

*Due to the threat of the Hunting ban at the time this was written

as cloth, brass catching the weak winter sun, springing open at exactly the right time, with a good brown hare a hundred yards ahead. Yes, this year will be a little different, but not all that different. Just as the bits and the stirrups have changed, so there will be other changes, but the core task will remain the same. Horses and hounds and other living creatures will still interact in ways as old as time, working for the countryside as part of the countryside. We owe it to such as this old hunter, to the saddler who made those slips, and to the children who are our future.

My young friend has hung up the bridles, and there is a small heap of spare straps to put away again. They will all find a job by and by. The antler and whalebone whips are back on their rack, and it is time for me to go. The old hunter escorts me to the gate. His eyes are wise and kind, his manner affable, and hope is in his every hoofbeat, for he has been listening to the combines, and he knows the smell of autumn.

IV

Our ratting pack has expanded its remit, and this was a day to spend in the woodlands, where we had been asked to attend to various quarry injurious to trees as well as other wildlife and crops. We were after rats, mink, rabbits and grey squirrels, and in order to remain strictly within the letter of the law,* that meant that rats and rabbits could be caught by the

*Refers to the Hunting ban passed a few months previously

dogs but mink and squirrels were to be shot. It was, however quite legal to flush any of our intended quarry to the gun, and so two of our members were carrying shotguns. These were Old Tom and Stanislaus, both very trustworthy under all circumstances. Tom is a foundation member of the Ratters, but we have not had Stanislaus with us for long, and nobody really knows how and when he came to join us. He works somewhere nearby; his English is fractured, his manners impeccable, and he can't half shoot. For dogs, we had the whippet, the labrador, a bunch of terriers and near-terriers, and "Dreadful" the dachshund.

Rain threatened, and the leaves, half-turned to autumn colours, had already been stripped off many branches, leaving the trees en deshabille. This was important for squirreling, giving us a better view. The dogs dashed about in the woodland, sending piles of leaves whirling, and fat grey rodents that had been busy burying acorns, beechmast and other delicacies were sent high into the trees, a starburst of silhouettes against the bare branches. If they tried to put the tree-trunks between themselves and our guns, one of us would run round to the other side of the tree to make them turn back. Tom and Stanislaus dealt with the targets above our heads, and the dogs picked up fallen squirrels and mostly retrieved them unless that dog was a dachshund. Sometimes terriers would squabble briefly over a dead squirrel before being diverted to more rewarding pursuit of the living, for there were rabbits to be evicted from brambles. Here, the whippet came into his own, tearing through the woods, twisting and turning through gaps that made you gasp as you watched him, lifting rabbit after rabbit in his tiny jaws. Then he would retrieve carefully, stepping high over the branches and trailing brambles, presenting each rabbit gently as if it were the rarest of jewels. The labrador, more of a career retriever, gave the job no reverence but plenty of gusto: here, take it, I'm in a hurry to get more.

Then the pond, round the edge of which there might be rats, in the middle of which there would be a labrador, and maybe we would find a mink? The whole team gathered around the pond, which is a large one, and the devil was in the dachshund, which with nose down was powering away at a speed which nothing with legs that short should be able to go. A chorus of "Oi" sounds followed him, and maybe a few other words as well. Stanislaus, what does that phrase mean? But the dachshund was honest, and, smashing into the thicket, fired out a fox, which Tom dropped to a single barrel and a quiet smile of satisfaction. The whole canine team piled into the 'worry' on the carcase.

Weary but happy is the path back, with squirrels, rabbits, several rats and the fox accounted for. The daylight is fading, and there is a promise of frost. We have the other part of the woodland yet to tackle, and we compare dates to see when we are all available, then say our goodbyes. The sky is red behind us as we turn for home.

V

The ferrets have not worked since April, and are overcome with excitement when they see their carrying-box. There is a moment of mayhem as they pour through the two entrances, and I have to extract the ones that are not coming today; then there are two in one compartment, and finally I manage to have one in each compartment, which is how it should be. Those left behind are hanging on the weldmesh sides of their pens and looking astonished that I could have been so foolish in forgetting them. Fortunately, ferrets are easily distracted, and the two rabbit halves that I give them soon claim their attention, while the lucky pair is loaded up with all the rest of the gear.

It is a short ride to this farm. The buries have been cleared prior to being gassed, and we have been told that we can ferret them as long as we are finished by the weekend. These are buries to shoot over: the ground is too hard to net, and the railway line is too close to bring a dog, which is a pity as she would have loved to have come. Not as easily bought off as ferrets, the dogs have been left staring dolefully out of the window at home. We will have to make it up to them later. Meanwhile, we have fitted the locator collars to our small furry helpers, checked that the receiver box is working, and into the bury slither the ferrets, like small furry snakes. Standing well back, we await results, and they are not long in coming, for the first rabbit is out almost straight away, and rolling over to the first shot. Before the echo has died away, the second rabbit is out and running along the hedgerow, to go to ground in a small separate bury further down. One of the ferrets emerges, puts her nose to the scent and follows. We don't want her down the other bury just yet, so she is gently intercepted and returned to the main one. At the same time, underground bumping tells us that her companion has found a rabbit and is having a full and frank exchange of views with it. The arrival of the second ferret persuades the rabbit to bolt, and over he goes, a nice fat buck to go with the doe rabbit that was shot first. The second ferret pelts out of the bury, runs to the dead rabbit and starts shaking it fiercely. Clearly she has a score to settle. We let her finish making her point, after which she is quite docile, and comes running across to see us. The other ferret is out now, and both follow our special call and run behind us for the short distance to the next bury. We would of course carry them if it were any distance away, but the 'girls' are full of excitement, and a short run won't do them any harm at all. If I had spent the time on these ferrets that I do on training my dogs, who knows what I might have achieved? Each will come to call and follow to heel – unless of course there are any distractions, for a ferret's mindset is much more that of a cat than a dog. Both follow scent as well as any hound, possibly better, and now the polecat ferret is giving an exhibition of coursing.

A rabbit has left the bury and does not want to go back down – I wonder why? – but does not want to bolt along to the next place of shelter. So it runs around the top of the bury, and the ferret is pelting after it as fast as she can go. She cannot catch the rabbit, and we cannot shoot until it bolts clear. If she were a stoat, to which she is distantly related, she would use exactly the same technique until she could latch on to the rabbit. Fortunately the rabbit elects to run at this point, and is shot. At once the ferret runs after the scent and seizes the dead rabbit, actually starting to drag it towards us.

A retrieving ferret – whatever next? Bizarre as it may sound, some ferrets will drag rabbits out of buries as well. As we always give them a snack before working them, they are not bringing the rabbits along so that they can eat them, though possibly they intend to store them with us for safe keeping until they are hungry again. Anyway, we are vastly amused at our small polecat spaniel, and gently relieve her of her burden before she tires. She has, after all, more excitement in store, for we have other buries for her to investigate.

Before long, the morning changes from cool to uncomfortably warm, and we agree that the buries by the pond will be the last ones that we tackle today. These are not as productive as the buries under the hedge, but after a lot of hard work by the ferrets, we extract one rabbit – and miss it! There is still one rabbit below, and the ferrets are determined to evict it, for they both slip down underground before we can pick them up. Above ground, I am captivated by the antics of a big yellow-striped dragonfly which is flying around me on crisp stained-glass wings. I am not sure if this is a territorial display or if he is hunting, but he is certainly a fine fellow, and his flying skills are second to none, He is here, and here, and there, and over yonder, and back again, with no apparent effort. Then the final rabbit bolts, and my attention is jerked back to he matter in hand.

It is quite hot enough to go home now. The ferrets are uncollared and offered a drink, which they accept eagerly, and we start on our way back. Out in the field is a group of crows - a 'murder' is the correct term – one of which has a lot of white on it. This is common with the crows on this particular farm. This crow's markings are exceptionally symmetrical, with the whole spread of primaries on each wing and all of the fan of tail feathers white. The crows walk heavily over to where we have lately been, hoping that we may have left some pickings for them.

We stop off at the farm office and confirm that the buries have been ferreted, showing the results. A few rabbits remain behind, but whether it is now worth gassing them is for the landowner to decide. Anyway, we have done our bit for the environmentally friendly operation, and have enough rabbits for our dogs, all the ferrets, and some for our friends as well. A good morning's work by any standards.

VI

This farm, an hour's drive from where I live now, was where I used to spend a lot of my childhood. Of course, it was very different then. Farmer X raised cattle by way of business, and a few point-to-pointers as a hobby. Indeed, I am sure that the only reason I passed my eleven-plus was due, at a critical point during my maths problems, to being able to look out of the examination room window to see one of his horses being exercised along the lane. Farmer X's fields were where we went blackberrying and mushrooming in season, and there were ponds for tadpoles and sticklebacks, newts, frogs and toads. I attribute my lifelong interest in Nature to the start I had, watching and learning, where the cattle grazed and the dragonflies hawked, in these very fields.

They are a sad sight now. Farmer X's son should have taken over the tenancy upon his father's death, but the farm went to auction, and poor Tom had to see the land being knocked down to the developers. But the developers could not get planning permission. In retaliation, they despoiled the land, churning great trenches across it, felling the avenue of limes, the rare cork tree, the monkey puzzle tree that fascinated us as young children. They bulldozed the air-raid shelters, the cattle-yards and the stabling, leaving rubble and rusting corrugated iron sticking up like broken teeth into the sky. They were stopped from doing any more, and subsequently went out of business, but the desecration remained, thirty years and more now.

The council awarded itself permission to build some housing along one edge, and a different developer built an estate near the factory that went up where we used to fish the stream, and gather hazelnuts each autumn. Travellers moved in, added to the mess, and moved on, and carcasses of burnt-out cars appeared where the hedges were once riots of honeysuckle and roses. Elsewhere, the land reverted to scrub, for land needs maintenance and husbandry in order to stay useful and comely. The dog and I picked our way through thistles, nettles, ragwort and great banks of bramble, keeping clear of the broken glass and twisted metal, and blessing the local dog-walkers for keeping the old footpaths open. Over at the allotments, I could see the only good use being made of what once was an incredibly beautiful farm.

The dog did not share my feelings, for here there were still rabbits to chase. A dog had to be fast and maybe a little lucky to catch any, for there was so much cover, but she was enjoying herself. The rabbits were clearly used to dog-walkers and slower dogs, for they did not bestir themselves to keep out of the way until the last minute, which would eventually lead to a very final kind of last minute for some. Once, there were hares here: I remember the village boys bringing them back, but their mothers would not cook them. Mine would, and other things too, for there were eels in the streams, and pike where the water ran deeper and sweeter. So I learned how to cook the wild meats, and gather the wild fruits, fungi and plants to go with them. You would not risk eating anything from these ponds now, if anything had survived the metal and glass within or the oil slick over the top.

There are no dog-walkers yet, for it is too early. I was tempted to walk by the river, but I daresay the sight of a stranger with such a likely-looking dog and at this hour might make the bailiff feel uncomfortable, particularly as I am now carrying a brace of rabbits. In the overgrown remains of the garden by the millpond, I can hear a pheasant crowing. Good to know that there are still one or two about. I can remember the excitement when a pheasant came home, for it was a rare and much-appreciated treat. How times change: now I eat pheasant every week, though it will always be something special. So I skirt the lane leading to the river and instead pick my way along where the irises and kingcups

still bloom, and the willow-herb, fireweed we called it, showed amongst
the debris of what once were good stone buildings. Then up by the bomb-
crater, through the new fence (developers put up doughty fences if
nothing else) and onto the track that leads to the road. I can see a fair way
up the road from here, and approaching is an old countryman on a
boneshaker of a black bicycle. He cycles incredibly slowly, but the old
rattletrap stays upright. He is dressed for rough outdoor work: an ancient
blue suit jacket (the trousers to which had long since shredded into
obscurity) dark brown trousers, worn tweed cap. We meet at the corner,
and recognise each other, for he used to be cowman here.

"Well if it isn't young Foxglove" he says, pushing his cap back as he
speaks. Then, seeing the dog, and the rabbits I am carrying, he grins me
a gappy grin, and asks if it isn't time I mended my ways? We exchange a
little news, and he invites me to call in at the allotment, where he might
have "summat to go with they conies". Of course, I give him the best one,
paunching and skinning it on the spot, as his hands aren't too good
nowadays, and in return I come away with a bag of vegetables. As we
stride off back to the vehicle, my mind is full of ghosts and shadows, and
questions that have no answers.

VII

Coming back a little later than anticipated from autumn hunting, I just had time to change my boots, collect a dog, and a bag of pigeons that had been shot the previous day, and set off for a friend's house. On the way, I picked a capful of mushrooms, which have been very good this year, along with other fungi. Toadstools of several varieties were clustered around the trees or half-hidden in the grass, and I wished that I had brought my camera. The rough rule for wild fungi is that for whichever ones are delicious to eat, there are some exactly like them which will see you off. I was well taught in childhood by a Swiss lady who was most knowledgeable about what could be eaten and what was better left, but even so, I only pick when I am certain.

Half of a small farm sale seemed to be stacked in the garden when I arrived – this was obviously clearing out the shed day, one of those periodic country rituals. "Your shed's like the Tardis" I told him. How on earth had all that come out of one shed? There was an armchair of the sagging-but-comfy school, a pile of coats and orphaned rubber boots, a long-net much chewed by mice, which was a pity, assorted snares and traps, an old-fashioned boiler for cooking up dog food, umpteen garden tools, some with woodwormed handles, partially used tins of paint, all the kind of necessary equipment which has to mature in a shed for an unspecified length of time before either being thrown out, mended or given away. "Did you bring a dog?" was his reply. I stood aside to show that the little chap was at my heels, his wise, ragged face already registering interest at the job he was about to do. I gestured him forward into the shed, and my friend started to move some sacks with a stick.

The first mouse shot out like a demented bumblebee, catching us all by surprise and doing a quick circuit of the shed before disappearing under the sacks again. Now the dog was up on his toes, quivering, all excitement. Sacks were lifted and mice were shifted, the little dog snapping them up from the floor, leaping up the walls after them, and snatching them out of the air. I stood by the shed door as backstop. There was a litter of blind baby mice inside an old cardboard box. What to do with those? Drowning was a horrible death. No, it had to be the dog, the most humane way of dealing with them. "I hate using poison," said my friend, "but sometimes you have to. This is better."

I asked if he had seen rats, and the answer was yes, since the wheat had been cut, rats had come into the garden but luckily not yet into the shed. He had some traps set which were checked twice a day, and would use poison as a last resort. Now that we had cleared the shed of both sacks and mice, he would have a few traps set there, too, in case any more came in. It was a good shed, large and warm, ideal overwintering for rodents.

The dog was staring hard at the armchair, standing in classic pose with one foreleg raised and his head on one side. Gingerly, I lifted the cushion and out pinged a mouse, which the dog snapped up in midair. He showed no more interest, though George then insisted we turned the chair upside down and beat his stick underneath it. Luckily that mouse hadn't built a nest yet. It isn't all that relaxing, sharing an armchair with a mouse.

George's lovely wife then came out with a tray, two mugs of tea and two wedges of her home-made fruit cake. She put the tray on the garden table, saw the dog and went back to cut another slice. He, meanwhile, had turned on the full charm of his amber eyes and was sitting up with one paw raised, rather like one of the more saccharine Victorian pictures. She said that she could never resist his eyes, and the dog, ever the gentleman, took his cake gently and wagged his tail, while I muttered about keeping his weight down. "He's like the poacher's dog" was her indignant reply, "all ribs…….." and she winked. We didn't finish off the saying, but I expect you have heard it.

While we were enjoying our elevenses and discussing the recent Brighton protest against the proposed hunting ban, which had been a great success, All Ribs pottered off on a tour of the garden. Knowing his manners were good, I didn't keep much of an eye on him, so I was taken completely by surprise when he jumped onto the garden table and presented me with a young rat. "That's one less to trap, then," said George, and his wife said that the dog had definitely earned another piece of cake. Happily, she cut one for each of us as well.

VIII

Down by the river, the mist has yet to yield to the morning sun, and there is no-one else to be seen for miles. Cattle graze in hulking groups, finding the coarse salt pasture much to their liking. Two people and three dogs are crossing the grey-green landscape, and the staccato cocking of a distant pheasant is the loudest sound. Marvellous.

We leave the footpath to cross a friend's land, hoping to avoid the cattle, but they come to see us, bouncing and kicking with excitement, and shedding copious quantities of a warm substance in which some dogs might be tempted to roll. We send the dogs forwards to safety – cattle can get nasty with dogs – and they remove themselves to the other side of the gate while we walk across to the stile. There ahead of us is the remains of a dewpond, now overgrown and providing an ideal habitat for rabbits and rats. A nod to the dogs and in they go. The black dogs are built for stamina; by contrast, the white dog is the shape for speed. That is not a clear definitive, for the black dogs have a deceptively fast turn of foot, while the white dog can work steadily, unrested, for half a day. Together they make a formidable team, as many a rabbit will testify.

The myxomatosis has not reached this part of the river yet, but it cannot be far away. A healthy rabbit bolts straight away, is turned by the white dog towards one of the black dogs, which misses by a whisker as the rabbit jinks and darts through the stock-fence into the hedge. A dog could waste energy by leaping the fence, but once the rabbit is in the hedge it is likely to be straight down a hole. Better to stick with the yellowing sedges, which, reading the demeanour of all three dogs, hold a second rabbit. This one takes a fair bit of rootling out, dogs bouncing all around it before it loses its nerve and bolts. We lose that one as well. No matter, for the dogs are all delighted with the fun they have been having, and it is always a pleasure to see them work.

Through the next field, we keep them to heel as a courtesy to the shepherd, for although the dogs are steady to sheep, and although he is likely to recognise them when seen up close, he might think they were strays if spotted at a distance – and stray dogs are bad news in a flock of sheep. The mist has thickened as the sun becomes stronger, and will burn off in another hour, but for now it is trapping scent close to the ground, and the dogs are crackling with excitement. We send them forward as soon as we leave the field by stile and dog-flap, and into the black muddy water by the hedge-corner they go. Mallard erupt indignantly, and the white dog stops and looks back at me. She is young, and not sure into which category they belong. Are they poultry, in which case not to be touched, are they pheasants, in which case they may be flushed but not coursed until the office is given, or are they miscellaneous, in which case she is permitted to catch them? The black dogs already know, and are running over to another group of ducks on the stubbles, so I give the white dog the nod, and she arcs across the land to reach them, sending them up in a scatter. She leaps and only just misses: I can hear her teeth clip together. This is environmentally friendly wildfowling, and she will soon get better at it.

We make for the edge of the field, and signal the dogs ahead of us. They sweep around into some rough ground which leads to a little copse, and suddenly the tempo goes up as they hit a hot scent and all three drop their noses and go hell for leather into the trees. We are ahead of the game, for we know that look, and we divide either side of the point of the spinney. I am too late to see what leaves, but it has left, no mistake about that, with two dogs one side of the wood and one the other. Within seconds, there are no dogs at all. Taking a good guess, we each move to a vantage point, and after a very few minutes, the white dog is in sight, black to the belly with mud and going hard towards the next piece of woodland. The mist is all but gone now, and the sun, still low, makes seeing difficult, when we catch movement two hundred yards away. Flickering up the hedge like witchcraft come the black dogs, soaking wet and trailing greenery, heads down, totally focused on the scent. They cannot run faster than the scent allows, and the sun is burning it off with the mist. The lee of the hedge is holding, but as they turn the corner into full sunshine, the last of the scent has gone. Their headlong gallop slows: they turn and cast in vain for that luscious smell, but it has disappeared along with its owner, whatever it could have been. Busily the black dogs part each blade of grass, searching, but there is no clue for them. They turn back and pick up the scent in the shadows and take it forward, but stop when it stops, raising their heads. We step up into their line of vision and call them, making much of them, for they have done well. The white dog comes slouching round the hedge from the other direction and joins us. She has not been slacking either, for she would have been exactly right to apprehend the source of the smell if it had come through the hedge.

Now we are undeniably hot, and the dogs have had good exercise, so we angle across in front of some more cattle, which are luckily too engrossed in cudding to get up and inspect us, to pick up the footpath again. Swans sail parallel to the path, decide we are no threat and glide away, shipping their paddles like oars, and far in the distance we can see the church spire and hear a kettle calling.

IX

The hunters came up from grass towards the end of July, at the same time as the barley went under the blade. We ride past the combines billowing dust and chips of straw, pouring golden grain into the attending trailers. What would our forebears have thought of such mechanisation instead of the hard, hot, backbreaking toil that made their harvests? How they would have marvelled at the rich yield, barely touched by blight or weeds, making an undreamt-of return for the sowing. Though few of us like the use of agricultural sprays, and most keep them to a minimum, their contribution to the modern harvest must not be underrated. Once, a farmer was lucky to get a two and a half percent return on seed planted, but now each field is able to yield tons (or even tonnes) of bright grain. The horses prance and sidle, snorting and rolling their eyes at the devouring machinery, little knowing that they are looking at what was once a horse's job. What would they have thought of the teams of oxen that plodded the weald just within living memory?

It seems not all that many years ago that I walked the crops and pulled wild oats by hand, instead of the farmer spraying. It was by no means an unpleasant job, though you certainly knew you had done it. I would start just before dawn and stop when the sun reached its zenith, interrupting the job only to feed and let the poultry out, and pick up the first eggs. Back to the fields, nearly up to my waist in the dew-soaked crop, gloved to protect my hands and wearing my dreadful old hat against the sun, I would pull sackfuls of wild oats in a few hours. These would then be fed to the hens, and a handful to the old mare, mother of winners and a winner herself in her day. Now she dreamed her days away in retirement, ribby and sway-backed from bearing foals, lop-eared and drooping of lip, a world away from the cheering crowds that had once lined the rails as she galloped home. She was a cantankerous old faggot, always had been, and though she accepted my offering of oats readily enough, I was careful of her.

In my parents' day and before, children had to do their bit on the farm too, and used to pick up the stones in the fields, leaving them at the headland in little piles. Little ones just about toddling would be helping, carrying one stone at a time. Truly, mechanisation has given many cause to be grateful, were they only aware. A child never dared say that it was bored in those days!

Out of the crop that is still standing, rabbits bolt or creep before the swinging blades to safety in the hedgerows. Sitting tight and relying on camouflage is not a wise option in this situation. Though the myxomatosis never really went away this year, there seem to be plenty of rabbits. It will be too hot to take a dog along the hedge by the time I have finished with the horse side of things, but I fancy I shall come back at dusk and see what there is about.

A rising mist half-covers the sun as the track takes the horses away from the toiling combines, and a yaffle swoops ahead of us, giving his cackling laugh. Though we are on walking exercise only, our tack is foamed from horse sweat, and the horses steam gently, the heat and gradient having given them quite enough to do. Soon they will be fit, and wait on the stubbles beside the dark woods in the pre-dawn chill while hounds flicker in and out of the trees. For now, we hack home, the first few flies already beginning to annoy our hunters as the rest of the world stretches and wakes. The horses will be washed down and fed, the sweat rinsed from their saddlery, then we humans will enjoy a quick cup of tea while they eat. Tack-room kettles are second only to tack-room crockery for antiquity and character, and spoons have a high mortality rate.

With the yard set fair and the day people arriving, we early birds head home for shower and changing, to join a working day that has no idea of the camaraderie and pleasure that the early morning ride brings. As I drive back along the dual carriageway, I can just about see the dust from the combines that will still be working, headlights blazing, far into the evening, doing their bit to feed us all.

X

Ladies and gentlemen, we are gathered here together in this draughty old barn to partake of a special wisdom, and none of us wants to be here, especially Old George, whose wisdom it is.

That's what I'd like to say. But in fact we just nod and exchange the usual greetings. I am here partly to act as interpreter, for George isn't big on communication, and partly to give the afternoon some structure. George is giving a Masterclass: we will all go away wiser and, I suspect, sadder.

This, then, is a fox snare, only we call them 'wires'. It is much stronger than you would think, because we don't want it breaking. This is the swivel, which must also be that strong. The wire must be free from kinks – stress metal and it snaps. Also, the loop must be free-running. See, this runs freely and this is its permanent 'stop' nine inches from the body of the snare (that's my bit – George just says it has to be 'yere').

This one is a self-locking snare, which is illegal. You need to see the difference so that you know. This is a 'tealer', and you can have them made like these or like those, or even as you see here, but George favours this sort.

George warms to his task and I have less to do. An air of depression hangs over the students – none of us wants to set any more fox snares than we have to, but if we can't use our dogs to catch foxes,* if we haven't got the hunt to call upon, we are going to have to use wires up until the hunts can get going again.

George has finished describing the mechanics of the snare, and we are on the vital information of where to set them. We must do our best not to catch non-target species, though if we do, it is a relatively straightforward matter to release whatever we have found in them. The fox must be caught around the neck, nowhere else. The wires, by law, should be checked daily, but George recommends twice daily. The wires must be secured strongly because you don't want a fox getting away with one round its neck. After all, it would be illegal to use a dog to hunt until it finds it, and you won't find it without a dog. You are actually quite limited in where you set a wire, if you are going to do so responsibly, and of course the ideal places are sometimes off-limits because of interfering idiots who would damage the snares out of spite. So you cannot control foxes using wires alone, though they will do a good job, and they work around the clock in all weathers for no pay in those places where we cannot use a gun.

Just as the wire never sleeps, neither does the trap. These are cage traps, which are the only legal ones we can use against foxes at present. George pauses to show us some illegal traps, for he has been trapping since Noah was a lad. This cage trap from George's collection has a small compartment at one end, the correct use of which is illegal now. A pair of live hens or similar would once have been put in the end cage to tempt a fox in. But anyway (with a nod at Ted the retired policemen) we aren't allowed to do that any more.

The best traps are this long or longer, and here are some different internal arrangements, this one being better than that because. These are the ways that you place and secure the traps, and if you sprinkle on a little of this, which is legal, you can bring a fox in, but not every fox, oh dearie me no.

A lot of them won't get in a trap no matter what you do by way of a 'welcome' mat, which means the wires do a better job. Oh, and if you reckon on your wires being vandalised, you wants to see what stupid folks

*Refers to the proposed Hunting ban

does with a trap; what with the cost and all you are much better off with the wires only it's handy to have both. We all nod.

George, who isn't half as sleepy and rural as he seems, gives us the lowdown on poison and gas, neither of which is legally in use at the moment but (with a wink and a finger pressed to the nose) certain substances are being tested by the government.

Stella the hippy, who owns three acres at the end of this lane and is much troubled by foxes after her free-rangers, winces. She has travelled all over the place, and she knows the realities of using these latter methods, especially the effect on non-target species which of course cannot be set free afterwards in the way they could if caught in a snare or cage trap. Stella has a big mongrel dog which deals with foxes instantly and terminally, and he isn't going to stop.

The afternoon passes quickly. Relatively few people have a George available to teach them what he has taught us, and sadly, there will be

many traps and snares set in the future, not all with the expertise that he has so generously shared here.

As we rise and start to pack up, he asks us sharply if we are getting our paperwork in order. Because when we catch these foxes, we still have to kill them, and that will mean the necessary licensing to own guns for those of us who do not do so already. We should all be applying for firearms certificates now, so that we can each have a pistol to kill the foxes we catch, this being one of the main legal exemptions for using them. For sure, there will be a great many more people who are going to need them until such time as we can hunt again legally.

George calls me over as we get ready to go. I start to thank him for his time, but he waves my words aside. He has a fox coming into his orchard after his birds, and while he could wire or trap it, he'd just as soon not unless there is no alternative. Do I think we could ask for hounds to come over as soon as possible?

XI

It is hard to remember, even though not that many weeks later, just how hot and dusty it was at this year's harvesting, the combines working late into the night, every night. Those of us who were involved in shooting the rabbits and occasional foxes disturbed by the great machines walked for hours, taking the shortest of breaks to slake our thirsts and replenish our cartridge supplies before returning to our task.

On one of the last evenings, I returned home tingling with sunburn, wearing a mask of dust caked into my skin and hair, itching from a thousand insect bites, and utterly exhausted. Yet dogs still have to be exercised, and it had been a long time since our morning walk.

Revived by a sandwich consisting of two doorsteps of wholemeal bread separated by half an inch of cold roast beef, horseradish and butter, the whole washed down with cold water, I whistled up the dogs to take them for a quick spin. Upon my return, all but one was left at home, for there was one more job still to do. Country people call it 'going out to see what there is'.

There are rabbits, foxes and other beasts which are this year's breeding and have never known life other than among standing crops. They will come along their usual routes because they know no other, and they have not yet altered their habits to suit their changed world. This is the time to watch for them, to see and to learn. This is the time to creep along the edge of the new stubble, to sit in the ragged shadow of the huge straw bales, and to see by the light of the moon which creatures will pass by, and how many.

The dog is there as my trusted companion and fellow hunter, her senses far keener than mine, her discipline absolute. She lies serenely at my feet, her nose and ears reading information that comes on the wind, her eyes detecting tiny movements at a distance far greater than I am able.

The gnats and swallows have retired to bed by the time that the landscape starts to speak to me. First the rabbits come, hopping slowly, sitting up to look around at their changed landscape. We have shot so many since the combining started, and there are many more. Reports are of myxomatosis starting its march across the county as it does every year, so those that we kill ahead of the disease will be the lucky ones. But for the moment, I just watch.

A flash of movement up by the far hedge catches the dog's attention as well as mine. A half-grown fox perhaps? Traditionally known as 'cubs' until the end of their first winter, these are as much cubs as nineteen-year-old humans are children, and a group of them has as much winsome appeal as a crowd of youths hanging around the off-licence. I need to know how many cubs, how many adult foxes, are trading through, and where. Over the next few weeks, a lot of people will be dedicating a lot of time to reducing these to an acceptable level.

The sudden movement resolves itself into the first-year fox that I was expecting to see: a fox that runs down the tram-lines in the stubble and then veers off through a hedge at what is clearly its regular run. The dog remains silent, but her hackles rise against my fingers.

A rabbit dashes past my feet, running terrified, its ears flat, eyes looking behind. I know what I will see next and there it is: a fine stoat that follows purposefully in its tracks, not hurrying, not dallying, nose to ground like a miniature hound. Unless something happens to the stoat, the rabbit is doomed, for the stoat will follow it above ground or under, a war of attrition that will end with the rabbit crouching in helpless despair, squealing its anguish, until the mustelid trademark, the bite to the back of the head, ends its ordeal.

Turning my eyes to another corner of the field, I see the black and white cat that is stalking something small. Maybe a quick death, maybe a long one, depending on the cat and whether it is hungry. After similar quarry comes the barn owl, but she kills swiftly, flopping onto the stubble and coming straight up again, then down and staying down for a moment, to tear and swallow her supper in rapid gulps. Then away she floats, silent and lovely.

I could have stayed out there all night, tired as I was. I had seen much

that would be of use, and the time had been well spent. I moved unobtrusively out of the darkness of the bales and trod softly up the headland, my dog another shadow behind me. The hedgerow joined the farm track to the bottom yard, vehicle and home, whence I could wash off the dusty evidence of my day, feed the dogs and finish off the horseradish with the help of the loaf and the rest of the beef. There was the possibility of a pint of bitter as well.

XII

It was still dark as I exercised the dogs, not pre-dawn but thoroughly dark. While the dogs attended to their ablutions, I enjoyed the sequinned sky, finding Orion's belt, then Orion himself, the hunter. The Plough hung beside, and Venus, the Morning Star, brighter than all the others, beckoned the dawn. Such was to be my morning: the hunter, the newly ploughed fields, the love of the countryside. I was taking someone fox-hunting for the first time.

Understanding the ways of nature is not an issue of town versus country, but rather a matter of closed minds and open ones. My friend is a Londoner, brought up in great hardship, but the core of his heart led him to the countryside. He is streetwise and quick-minded, missing little.

I met him as arranged and we drove to the meet, one of the last autumn hunting mornings.

Woodland hunting is much listening and less seeing, yet there is still plenty to see. A touch of frost, dragged green where an animal had passed, cobwebs filigreed with dew. The pack tumbled eagerly out of their transport; horses fidgeted and clicked their bit-rings. Last-minute adjustments to girths and gloves, the briefest of notes on the horn, and the professionals rustled past to begin their day at the office. We, observers and helpers, followed their tracks and took up our places.

In the rank undergrowth, scent lay differently from the open rides, and hounds were working diligently. Foxes were afoot, and a fine fellow broke cover between us, looking first at my friend, then at me, before gliding across into the next thicket. Tally-ho over! The pack that had roused him poured across after him, precisely on his line, the huntsman all concentration but still finding time to bid us a quick greeting.

The whipper-in waited just so on a likely corner. "Look at that for a photograph," said one of the followers softly, and what a photograph it would have made. The whipper-in sat on a grey horse, lit from behind by arrows of rising sun, mist rising from the thawing ground, steam rising from the warm body of the horse, eternity and the beauty of hunting encapsulated in one brief heartbeat of time.

Then the fox flurried out from further down, having sat in his thorned refuge, the huntsman wheeled around on his bay horse to be right for his pack, and hounds streamed joyously in the wake of their fox. But scent is far more complex than we can ever guess at, and the pack was brought to its noses in the rank woodland.

One of the footfollowers' dogs gave the reason, stretching upwards to drink the failing smell of fox. When a tall dog scents upwards (and not many will) or a man on a horse can smell the taint of fox, it means that scent is rising quickly on the air. "Here's to the hound with his nose upon the ground" is the toast, and even the best of hounds cannot follow scent which has climbed out of his reach.

We drew a sun-warmed patch of bracken and pushed out a small dark fox that was bustled round for twenty minutes or so before going to ground. My London friend had already commented on the distinctive voice of one of the hounds, and how it was always followed by the main cry of the pack. Obviously this was a staunch finding hound, to whom the others rallied, knowing that he or she would be right: equally obviously, my town friend was a natural hunter for having noticed this.

And indeed we heard that high yodelling cry again, the crash of hound music that joined it, and another lively hunt followed, while the first fox was being dug out and shot. Where there are these many foxes, the numbers must be reduced drastically before winter begins to bite.

Hounds hunted on into the valley and up the other side while we enjoyed the power and drive of their working, the neat unobtrusive figure of the huntsman, helping without interfering, the whipper-in everywhere at once, doing a hard job and making it look easy.

You could follow the progress of the fox if you only took notice of the crowing pheasants, the quacking of disturbed ducks, the cursing of the crows, a pause, then the traitorous magpie cackle, dry as dust. A touch of the horn in the valley, the whipper-in's voice on the hill, told us that soon they would be on their way back. The sun was warm, the frost gone, three hours had slipped by. My friend had to go back to London, though he would stop for a mug of good coffee first.

Life is too short to drink lousy coffee, or to miss a woodland hunting morning before the opening meet. Well, what did you think of it? You want to come out again as soon as possible? So do all of us, and you will be made most welcome.

Winter

I

Our Saturday morning ratting club is a model of political correctness. Among our members are several different ethnic minorities – there is even someone from Hampshire – all ages from pensioners to single figures, several colours especially when we've just finished, and probably a number of gender orientations, though good manners preclude the discussion of these within the membership.

Dogs range from those of impeccable pedigree to those who were only related to their littermates on their mother's side. Some are vertically challenged, some intellectually so, a few have missing teeth, and others are paragons of youth and beauty – and that's just the owners. We have a couple of pipe smokers – Old Shag if you must – several who bring alcohol in hip flasks, and one who injects insulin. All in all a typical group of Sussex Ratters.

We meet by arrangement at a series of venues in the countryside, for although there are even more rats in the towns, you do get a better class of rodent out in the fields and farm buildings. Dress is essential but informal: any kind of upper raiment will do, but nether garments need to be tied below the knee – usually with baler twine, that indispensable item of country equipment, though a few of our wealthier subscribers wear gaiters (including me – I had some for Christmas last year). Boots are of leather. You might think that wellingtons would be just the job, coming higher up the leg and all, but do you realise what a decent pair of wellies costs these days? No way do you want a rat bite puncturing one of those. We who work and play out of doors in all weathers need comfortable wellies, none of your garden centre cheapies, and anyway, leather protects the feet from rat bites, not to mention the odd over-enthusiastic terrier. So we wear anything from climbing boots to Doc Martens, trousers tucked into socks, and that essential twist of string around all of it.

This time of year we meet in the very early morning, while it is still dark, for with the aid of a torch it is possible to find rats out in the open where the dogs can get a good run at them. Rats running along beams above us can be knocked off with a stick, but otherwise the brandishing of sticks is discouraged, for we have dogs to do the rat-catching. Only amateur dogs shake the rats: these veteran ratters snap them up and drop them dead in one movement, faster than you can see. They don't waste time shaking one rat when they could be catching another and another.

Mostly terriers here: there's a brace of lakelands that will be going out with the hunt later, a patterdale, a pair of Jack Russell types and a bedlington (he's the one with the champion pedigree). There is a fine whippet from coursing stock, and a staffie which is a bit on the leg for KC registration, and generally reckoned to have a bit of Irish mist about him. I've brought two lurchers.

This is a lawn meet, which means that although we get going straight away so not to miss the benefit of the darkness, at eight o'clock the farmer comes out with egg and bacon butties and mugs of tea. We are good boys and girls, and wash our hands thoroughly with antiseptic soap before getting stuck into this glorious repast, because rats carry some very nasty diseases that we'd just as soon do without.

Our smallest members, a brother and sister seven and nine years old respectively, would soon tell us off for any lapse in hygiene. They also count up the rats and keep the game book for us. Monty is in charge of the camera, on account of it's his, and he takes a photo or two at the end of every ratting session, which goes in the diary as well. I'm not sure what we will do with our hunting records, but they may be a historical document one day.

Jan is the club nurse, and a real nurse as well. She deals with any nips sustained by the dogs, and is responsible for the ruthless disinfecting of any grazed skin on humans. This causes a certain amount of extraneous noise, which is another reason for delaying medical treatment until the breakfast break. We then share the crusts around the waiting dogs, the whippet shivering pathetically with apparent starvation, and Monty looks as if he might light his pipe, which is a signal to get going before he does.

And then the terriers start circling each other, there is the hint of a growl here and a lifted lip there, and we'd best get back to the job in hand sharpish before the little devils start a fight. The lakelands are off to do their day job, and Ahmed is leaving to go coursing, but still plenty of us

are left to get another couple of hours in, starting with the log pile now that we can see what we're doing.

Old Tom is on top of the corrugated iron with a ringside view, and George is moving some logs that his bedlington was marking. Careful man, you'll have the lot down! Out shoots a rat: there is a holloa on the other side from Bethany which denotes another bolter, the bull terrier is squealing with excitement as only a bullie can, and endeavouring to dig through the foundations, pulling at the wooden sleepers with his immense jaws. The whippet leaps four foot into the air to nip a rat off the side of the shed, and one of my dogs has knocked over a plastic barrel, diving inside to take another rat.

We pack up with a splendid tally of rats, and it is starting to rain, so I don't know about the photography, but Monty is confident. I have just got time to go home, swap dogs and see if I can find the hunt. We'll probably miss the meet, but I have an idea where they will be.

II

Among the downs lie many tiny hamlets, clusters of cottages around a farmhouse and very little else. There will be a letterbox set in a pillar, maybe a layby along the winding track, and very often, a beautiful, tiny church. Glistening with local flint, spire showing high across to the next one, these exquisite holy buildings are now at risk from falling congregations and the inevitable decline that Time writes even in stone. And it was near to one such that the hunt met on a bitter, bright day, the frost seeping out of the ground just in time for us to have a few hours out with the hounds.

Hunting and the clergy has been inextricably linked for longer even than these churches know, and for centuries, the keeping of fine hounds and hawks was as much a part of outdoor religion as hymns and prayers were performed inside consecrated walls. And so in respect of this and other loyalties, the hunt donated its income from the day's followers to the support of this downland church, funds for its restoration being urgently required. Then we moved off up a long, steep slope, leading to others longer and steeper, as is the way of the Sussex downs.

We are still learning so far as following a trail* is concerned, and it is very difficult for all of us, particularly the animals. It is harder for them to settle into a rhythm, which used to come easily with real hunting, but we are doing our best. Only a few people know where the trail starts, and fewer yet where it leads or how many challenges it poses along the way, doubling back on itself or crossing from cover to cover in the manner of a proper quarry. The horses are barely warmed up when the first fence looms, a downhill approach over a decent post-and-rail, which those who are jumping balloon over, giving plenty of room because the landing is downhill also. Around the side come the cunning who know their country, and are not jumping for one reason or another: a treasured old mare who can no longer be risked over fences but loves to see hounds leads the way. She has the genuine hunter build of 'a face like a Duchess and a farewell like a cook' and is still a great beauty. There are many ways to enjoy being out with hounds. Across the way, footfollowers have found a good vantage point, leaning on their sticks in the way they always have, and discussing hunts past on this land. I remember as if it were yesterday the blue fox that came out of that covert along with a yellow one, 'red' foxes having a wide range of colour variation. One went right and one left: the yellow fox went to ground in the next plantation and the pack, coming back, picked up the drag of the blue. They bustled him out and took him across the opposite hill and then he turned downhill and pulled up the side we were on, while we all stood still so as not to turn him. I truly think he did not know we were there. I have seen many colours in foxes but never a one quite so blue, and he came so close to me I could have taken two steps and touched him. Across the ridge he went, then down the next slope and heading back towards the covert from whence he had come, hounds now half a length from his brush, and yet it was not his time on this occasion, for he made it into the woods as the lead hound opened her jaws to take him, and he escaped. A film crew had been with us for the day, bored, cold and smoking endlessly, then had this amazing footage presented to them. I wonder if they realised how lucky they had

*First season after the Hunting ban

been, placed here just right and seeing such an unusual fox, and so close. There were foxes for several years afterwards in this area that had blue in their coats, though none that were blue all over, so he must have had at least one breeding season afterwards.

The air drops chill as we turn for home, full of memories and knowledge of the land, and the little old church stands proudly as we come towards it again, full of memories also, and a little better for our passing.

III

Which do you believe: the barometer, the television weather forecast, the internet, the piece of seaweed, the aches and pains? Look at the sky, deceptively benign, test the wind, hardly there, see a bank of cloud so far away that it seems irrelevant with the breeze before it. Will you be wetter from perspiring inside your waterproofs than from leaving them off? Wet tweed, wet boiled wool, are each warm and will dry with your body heat unless soaked through, in which case they will take days to dry. Are wet feet inside wellingtons more comfortable than wet feet inside honest leather? Is the state-of-the-art new 'breathable' boot lining all it is cracked up to be? Are Old Bert's two supermarket carrier bags, one on each foot before it goes into the boot, just as good? So run the thoughts as we don our various waterproofs or not, depending on how lucky we feel. One thing for sure: at some point of today, every one of us will be wrong.

When I was involved in another world, this is what we would have called a 'fool's flying day'. Calm and serene, it would last long enough for a friend to be telephoned, a small aircraft to be brought, blinking, out of its hangar, pre-flighted, fuelled, the flight planned and necessary paperwork passed to interested parties. By the time all the preliminaries would have been completed, clouds would have gathered and a vicious crosswind manifested itself. In that circumstance, we could make our way, growling, back to the clubhouse and drink coffee, but today we must take whatever comes.

The technology of the beating line has not changed all that much in the last couple of hundred years. A stick, maybe a flag, a well-behaved dog, would fit the picture at any pause in the history of the driven shoot. The clothes are a little different, the gamekeeper just as tense, and thank goodness for the invention of the chocolate bar. We step carefully through the dew-wet cover-crop, birds scurrying ahead of us into the tree-line. Steady is the way, keeping them on the ground until the right time for the flush, then sending them aloft in small groups. The sun beats down on us, making those in waxed waterproofs most uncomfortable.

The tweed and wool is more forgiving at this stage, heavy but breathable. The wide-brimmed Australian hat is a nuisance: too big to be stowed in a pocket, unlike the flat cap. Now we are in the trees, slowly uphill through the thorn thicket. You thought the bramble was difficult until the briar caught and held you, thought the hawthorn a penance until you met the blackthorn. The old-man's-beard might be pretty but it has the arresting powers of steel hawsers, and the slope is beginning to tell on us. The woods are warm, and see us loosening fastenings. No noise is heard except the tapping of sticks, and the 'keeper's voice telling the left flank to come across. The birds are flushing nicely.

By the second drive, we are all steaming under our clothes, and those who set out in mere waistcoats and optimism are by far the most comfortable. But the erstwhile smiling sky is now a rolling grey, and the wind has got up mightily. Now the Australian hat is a nuisance with the wind under its brim; there must be wind in Australia, so what is the trick of keeping the thing on?

A smatter of rain whips across the line as we stride into the open: coats are pulled to, and towelling scarves appear from pockets. The temperature has dropped a couple of degrees and we are all as comfortable as each other, but not for long. The next block of forestry is a long way away as the wind rises and the world turns grey with sheeting rain.

 Some of the dogs bolt for cover, and are not called back. Remaining coats are fastened quickly, and the man in shirtsleeves laughs, for what else can he do? Kipling knows the sort of warrior it took to 'break the

British square' and it takes more than torrential rain to break the beating line, though it is certainly more ragged as we gasp in the wind that takes our breath, and roar with mirth at what is happening to us.

Now the Australian hat comes into its own: wedged firmly on its owner's head, it throws water contemptuously off its brim and well clear of the coat-collar. Now you realise how important measurements can be: you do not want a coat whose hem drips water accurately into your leggings, which then funnel it into your boots. Gaiters are the superior article for channelling water from trouser leg to ground without involving footwear. The coat collar should turn up and fasten – and with that, we are on grey-out as the wind howls a crescendo and starts throwing hail at us. We are almost at the trees now, and the 'keeper has mercy on us, for after all, nothing will fly in this. The welcoming forestry closes behind us, and we turn, joking and dripping, to watch the hail settling glistening white on the coloured leaves left from autumn. Wet dogs return, and look for somebody to shake against.

We squelch through the next drive as wet as each other, and by the next, the sun is out again and steam is rising in a cloud from all of us. When we break for lunch, those of us pessimistic enough to have brought a change of clothing hop about peeling off wet gear and replacing it with dry. The 'keeper's wife spirits away a small group of children to find some towels and dry things for them, not the first time that she has done this over the years.

The rest of us pass flasks around and dig into packed lunches, while dogs insinuate themselves between likely friends, and tout for crusts. A pleasant smell of wet dog, waxed jackets and steaming tweed mingles with the soup and sandwiches. The Australian hat is quite dry, and ready for anything the afternoon can provide; bearing in mind this country's facility for providing four seasons in one day, we could likely get it all over again.

IV

Even the lure of hound and horn, or gun and pheasant, doesn't keep us away from the rabbits for long. I had been hunting, and my colleague had been shooting, all day, but a change of clothes and a good meal set us up for a night's lamping with the rifle.

Last time we came here was just after harvest, and despite our having removed an appreciable haul of rabbits, there were plenty out again this night. Into the first field then with a pause and a lurch through the gateway, and we were ready for action.

This came almost at once with a long shot well taken (I can say that as I wasn't shooting) though the next rabbit fell down the rabbit hole it had been sitting beside when it was shot, necessitating an arm in up to the shoulder to retrieve it. That meant we lost sight of the first rabbit somewhere between the end of the hedge and the telegraph pole. Unless they are considerate enough to fall white side up, they can be very hard to see at night, and we wanted to pick up all the rabbits that we shot, for there were hungry mouths waiting for them. In any case, I hate waste, and there are always plenty of takers for our rabbits.

Meanwhile, there was a rabbit running in which looked good for a shot, but it hopped a few paces and paused, hopped and paused again, never staying still long enough. It continued to hop and pause all the way into the woods, where we had to give it best, but no matter for there were plenty more.

Two together: both sat and both shot. That's more like it. Swing around away from the road – can't shoot that way and of course there is always a little pocket of rabbits where you can't shoot – and by Jove, is that our first rabbit? Yes it is, so not wasted after all.

The next rabbit is absolutely huge, and I wondered if it was pregnant, which is possible even this time of year. Later inspection showed that it was simply an enormous rabbit, stacked full of fat around its internal organs. We shot several like it, though none quite as big, from this field, and I wondered if they had been plundering the gardens of the large houses nearby.

Then on to more rabbit-sized rabbits, at least for this part of the country. The further north you get, the larger the rabbits seem to grow. Here in Sussex, three pounds seems to be an average weight, though wetland areas tend to have smaller rabbits.

Eight rabbits later, we leave the field and put the rifle away for the short trip along the road. Then we are off-road again, first of all beside a private drive (two rabbits, one involving quite a long walk to pick it up because the land is too wet to drive upon) and then into a rather charming natural basin in the pasture.

We are keeping away from the buildings as there are guests staying tonight and we do not wish to disturb them. The rifle is quiet enough, but they might find the lights or vehicle noise irksome.

In common with much Sussex land (but rather confusing for the incomer) the bottom of the grassy basin is dry but the top is wet, so we drive around the bottom part and shoot some rabbits off the sides. That doesn't take long, and we have two more fields to do, so off along the track and over the cattle grid, sharp right and mind the cat that comes out of nowhere straight for the only moving vehicle in its vicinity. The cat's shadow is huge – is this how the 'puma' tales start? Now we are in a vast flat field which at first glance looks perfect to run a dog on, but is not – the surface is treacherously rutted and fissured. The vehicle takes no harm, and if it did it could be mended, but we wouldn't risk a dog here.

A little owl sits on the ground, as they often do, and presently flies and lands a little way on, to sit and meditate from a different viewpoint. Cutting across the furthermost corner of the field flits a roe deer: there are many here, and a few fallow as well. The old woodland suits them.

It suits rabbits, too, and there are plenty, the grass just long enough to make them sit. A lifted ear or a raised head is all we need, changing direction to keep the background safe, and picking them off. Sometimes we find a rut the hard way, with a tooth-rattling jolt, and the rabbit we are after is off, away to safety. Easing through the gap where we almost grounded back in the summer, we see rabbits dotted across the final field, most of which pick up their skirts and run as soon as they realise we have joined them.

Even so, we manage a respectable number, though not as many as in the previous field because the grass is shorter and the rabbits do not care to linger. Two more down the side of the drive, and then off to the top of the hill for a last look around.

There is a firework display in the town, but the noise carries all the way here. We need not have been concerned about disturbing the neighbours. The night itself is clearing and the temperature dropping; maybe there will be a frost after all.

We are pleasantly tired after a long, happy day and the morrow will be devoted to plucking pheasants and skinning rabbits, after which, charged with virtue, we might well take the dogs out and see what we can find.

V

Short of daylight, with an afternoon power cut to speed us nightwards, I was plucking pheasants by candlelight when a friend arrived, glowing and ragged-haired from the wind, and with a sack of pigeons newly shot. What a day he had enjoyed, shooting over the winter rape, and ready to share his bounty, as is the way of the countryside. I had a surprise for him, too, and I waved him into the game larder and out of the wind. Two big Norfolk hares were hanging from one of the beams, another friend having lately passed by on his way back from coursing. He fields a five-year-old bitch, a flighty, scatty creature, always in the pink of condition, and everybody's friend. The world is always a little emptier after a visit from this whirlwind of a greyhound, still full of beans even after the long journey and six testing courses.

They had left with three brace of partridge, the last that we will have this season. A hare and a mug of coffee later, my pigeon-shooting friend was on his way, having kindly offered to leave a brace of pheasant by a farm that he would be passing, and I knew that he would be leaving a few woodpigeon as well. From the same farm, I had lately received a string of good strong English onions, and some fresh beetroot, earthy and sweet. If you simmer the beetroot slowly, and then serve cold in slices with slivers of raw onion, you have the perfect accompaniment to cold game.

I put a few pheasant tail feathers aside for a friend's kitten to have as playthings, and moved on to the woodies. Their subtle colours of powder grey and soft buff were much more in keeping with our countryside than the brightness of the pheasants, yet who does not thrill to see these glamorous fowl stalking through the woodlands? It does not take long to pluck pigeons, but while I was still so occupied, the lights came back on, and another friend arrived from the great outdoors, bearing a mixed bag of vermin. Grey squirrels for the ferrets, possibly their favourite meal, a couple of jays and a pile of crows. He had rather considerately left the rat behind, rats being one of the few quarry species that don't get recycled as food here. The other rats would soon eat it, if a fox did not find it first. The squirrel tails and the bright blue pin-feathers of the jays would be reborn as fishing flies, and the ferrets would eat the rest. Have some pigeons to take home? I was beginning to feel like a clearing-house for countryside products.

The dogs appeared politely at the door, not scrounging, you understand, but just wondering what the rabbit situation was. When rabbits are being skinned, a dog might be given a lucky rabbit's foot to take away and crunch up. Maybe not so lucky for the rabbit, which had four of them and still got caught. We have a large pot which will hold three rabbits and lots of vegetable odds and ends, maybe some windfall apples which we were given a while back and put in the freezer, and there you have a proper meal for dogs. The cooked rabbit will be carefully boned, cooked bones being dangerous for dogs, and then served with a thick vegetable broth. Many a family, when I was a child, would have been glad of a meal like that.

The kitchen is warm and welcoming, supper almost ready when I come in. Friendship, sharing, a little work and a lot of fun. The dogs cluster around me, interfering with the business of slippers, and I feel the timelessness of our country ways warm as a coat around me.

VI

A sliver of sickle moon in a clear sky sparkled with stars, a bitter frost: I love mornings that start like this. The diesel engine is loud in the pre-dawn hush, and as I crackle to a halt across the cobblestones, my headlights catch a long face looking out over the half-door, waiting for me. A low chuckle greets my arrival.

The stable bolt is stiff with frost, the orange light of the low-watt bulb only just enough. Inside, the stable is warm, the bed banked high at the edges and deep in the middle. Other long faces appear over doors, and there is the grating noise of hoof on concrete where someone gets up, scraping the bedding to the floor. They soon lose interest, knowing I am not for them. Under the rugs, the horse is warm and sweet-smelling, his clipped coat shining.

Pleased to see me, he hinders my every move by adding a nose to it, huge black-rimmed nostrils covered with velvet. There are big square teeth under the nose, plucking delicately at my coat. I warm the bit briefly in my hands before easing it gently into his mouth: he has beautiful manners, opening his mouth gently to receive it and lowering his head for the crownpiece to be slipped over his ears. These are outlined in black as well, with cream fluff inside.

I have flicked a soft brush briefly over his body, and taken the shavings out of his mane and tail, leaving the undermost rug over him to keep his saddle area warm. The saddle itself fits over a sheepskin pad, to dull the effect of icy leather and lessen the chance of a bucking fit when I settle into it. No need for the fluorescent gear this morning, for we are lucky enough not to be going off his owner's land, which is why I can ride by moonlight. My hat is cold on my head, and I wind my scarf tighter.

He clops out of the stable and pauses for me to close the door. Then we walk over to the wall which will serve me as mounting block. I am permitted one-eighth of a second to climb aboard, and I have too much sense to sit directly into the saddle, instead taking my weight on my knees while he ducks and sidles. Then I ease down into it, flinching at the temperature, for although there are sheepskin pads for riders as well as horses, I have never been able to afford one. Maybe this winter I will. Despite the cold, he is already foaming onto the bit, playing gently with it to show what a light mouth he has. Then a snort and a spin as a dark shadow arrives and turns itself into his owner's brindle greyhound. "You beggar, how did you get out?"

Please take me with you, oh please, says every line of the greyhound as she stretches low on her forelegs and licks her lips in supplication. I do not really want her company as, charming beast that she is, she is far less well-trained than I like a dog to be. But here she is, and I am aboard, and to take her back and find somewhere to shut her in will upset my not-all-that-safe conveyance, who is presently in the best of moods. "Come on, then."

She dances with delight, lashing her long tail, then sets off ahead of us. We clip down the drive at a swinging walk that could change to anything else very quickly, then, halfway down, turn right, cross the ridge, through the gap in the hedge and into the first field. This is deep enough after the recent rain to keep us to that athletic walk, and mist rises opaque from the earth to meet the lightening sky. The cold is burning my face and ungloved hands: I never did like riding with gloves on.

The bit-bars clink and an ear comes back to query. "Okay" I say, which is enough to have us trotting, and we trot along the fringe of the sixty-acre, down the track to the woods, and thence into the gloom of the trees. The graceful hound beside us capers along, nearly in the way, as unseen things patter off through the dead leaves either side of us. The horse's breath and mine rise like smoke above us.

We leave the wood on an uphill gradient, breaking out quite suddenly into light and the most amazing crimson dawn. Shot-silk across the sky, the shepherd's warning is a gasp of utter beauty that lasts for maybe five minutes until the clouds arrive to obscure it.

It seems that we have had the best of the day. The mist is rising thickly now, but not so dense that it obscures a fox going about its business, or a greyhound accelerating towards it. She is quickly into another belt of trees, and I can follow the Doppler effect of her progress by a receding noise of cackling pheasants, then the harsh nasal tones of an indignant mallard on the lake. Meanwhile, the horse and I are on the gallops, and he oils into his higher gears like the precision machine that he is. The scenery is a blur, my eyes and nose are streaming, the rhythm of his hooves is steady and good, his ears are pricked like twin gunsights ahead of me, and he is going well within himself.

He would like to go faster, but it is not yet the time. Just as I sit up and lighten my contact to slow him, a softer but more urgent galloping heralds a greyhound – the same one we started with, thank goodness – arriving at top speed behind us. She brakes in a flurry of long gangly legs and whirling tail, causing me to have to survive a mighty sideways leap and a fairly gentlemanly buck.

It is too lovely a morning for the short phrase that I have just uttered. She drops her ears and wags her tail, grinning, knowing how fond of her I am, knowing that I do not mean it. Then she bends her tiger-striped back in a hoop and speeds away home, for home is just away to the left, though I will be going the long way round to let Sir relax and cool down.

Sir does not want to relax and cool down. He wants to dance sideways, to flick his bit up and catch it, showering me with foam, to drop his head and lift his back, to give a noise that is half-grunt, half-squeal, cocking an ear behind to see if I am taking him seriously.

In response, I throw him the reins and call his bluff. Satisfied, he relaxes again, and the flurry of goldfinches across his bows causes only a minor mince and dive. They settle in a small tree, like living leaves, but are barely arranged before they all fly away again. What a jewel of a morning.

He swaggers back into the yard, which is all bustle and Radio 1, in contrast to the quiet of my arrival. His stable is ready with enough warm water in the bucket to take the chill off, and his breakfast is ready in the feed room.

He is almost dry, and modern rugs wick away the sweat from a horse that has done some work, unlike in my day when we had to dry them off with straw and stable rubbers. It is the work of moments to set him fair, check his legs and feed him; later he will be thoroughly groomed, though not by me, for I must away to work.

The cold is raw now, with none of the dry sparkle of earlier. I exchange information with those who need to know, and see that the greyhound is in the tack room, lying on a horse rug by the small electric fire. She flaps a long tail at me.

I have rinsed the bit and hung up the bridle ready for cleaning, stripped the sweaty sheepskin pad from the saddle along with the girth, and left them over the saddle horse from where they will receive appropriate attention later in the day. The saddle itself is already on its way to another horse. "I warmed it up for you," I say.

VII

We went mob-handed, which is the only way to tackle rabbit buries of these dimensions. On sandy soil, rabbits dig deep homes and can be reluctant to bolt, giving the most determined ferrets the run-around, or else just facing into a blind tunnel and refusing to budge. The hedgerow we were about to ferret had seen better days, which was all to our advantage as it was ragged and open, with easy access for net-setting. Pock-marked with rabbit holes, it ran in one continuous bury for three hundred yards until it met another hedge at right-angles, which was also one interconnecting bury along the full length. Satellite buries fed into it from the fields, often more than a hundred yards from the main warren. To my certain knowledge, no-one had attempted ferreting it in years, and who could blame them?

Six people, three hundred purse nets, four long-nets, three dogs and fourteen ferrets was the sum of our endeavour. The purse-nets were set on the satellite buries and along the more open of the rabbit-holes in the hedgerow, while the long-nets bisected it at intervals where the ground allowed. Ferreting is most usually the pastime of people who prefer to be alone, or just with a dog and one trusted companion, so to operate in a group, or even find sufficient compatible people to create a group, was unusual. We had left warm beds in the dark, loaded our vehicles in a light scatter of snow shower, and now we were trying to set nets in a biting wind, while the dogs circled the warren and told us: Here, and Here and Here. At the same time, the dogs studied each other from under their brows, for ferreting dogs are not pack animals, disliking the presence of other dogs when they are working, and often even when they are not. The sheep came over the hill to look at us, but the dogs ignored them, as properly-trained working dogs will.

It took us more than an hour to set all those nets, and then we huddled in the back of the largest vehicle, drinking coffee and eating our breakfast sandwiches, while the bury recovered from the alien sounds and scents of our net-setting. The dogs politely accepted crusts, each eyeing the others to make sure that the distribution was fair. Fourteen ferrets, fourteen transmitter collars, six locator boxes: so much technology against the rabbit. We placed three of the locator boxes so that we had one either end of the stretch we had netted – barely a hundred yards even with all those nets – and one in the middle, and three of us took one each. We lined observers at strategic points on each side of the hedgeline, and into the bury poured a river of ferrets, cataracting down into the dark, one seamless sinuous curve of pale fur. The rabbits were taken by surprise so that they could not flee or hide below ground, and the only course of action was to bolt in front of that torrent of predators. So fast did they hit the nets that some pelted clean through them, to be scooped up by the dogs as they ran. Some came out of un-netted holes and dived back into netted ones, causing human acrobatics as we pulled them out, sometimes at arm's length, sometimes lost completely despite our efforts. The dogs leaped and dived and coursed and fetched back, and we piled the caught conies in groups, or hung them in branches to collect later. Ferrets showed at the satellite buries, but no rabbits bolted from there, choosing instead to run up and down the hedgeline as they usually will. This time it did not help them, for our fire-power was too great. The dogs bounced over the longnets and the rabbits ran into them, some so hard that here and there the poles leaned over, pulling down the top-cord, and we had no time to adjust them because the rabbits were everywhere needing attention.

Gradually we slowed down after the initial rush, watching the dogs marking above where the ferrets were below, and every now and then a rabbit would exit in a hurry to show us where the ferrets had moved, if the ticking of the locator boxes had not already done so. We started to collect ferrets up as they came to the surface, for we did not want to risk losing any. The little creatures had worked so hard, running along the deep underground tunnels, and they would be ready for a drink and a rest. Thirteen came readily to hand, and we swung the locators back and forth the length of the netted area to try and pick up the missing one. Not a cheep. We backtracked and went forward, but we could not get a signal. Perhaps the collar had malfunctioned. Then I saw a rabbit bolt, and another, and we hurried to the spot where surely our missing ferret would be. Still no sound on the locator, but the black dog was waving her tail and pawing at a rabbit hole, and shortly afterwards, the ferret showed there. She came to hand straight away, having now finished her work, and as the weather was worsening again and it would take well over an hour to pick up the nets and paunch out the catch, we decided to call it a day. Collecting up rabbits from where we had left them as we worked showed that we had caught quite a haul, and many more than we had anticipated from this difficult place. We had made a good start, and though it was close to the end of the ferreting season, we would be back.

VIII

Waking up to the sound of rain on the windows had become almost a daily experience, and this morning was no exception. I left home after the usual chores in steady drizzle, which turned to lashing rain as I crossed the river, this being already well over its banks. The water meadows would be living up to their name, then. What a shame we could not have had a dry day for the Children's Meet. Country children, however, are made of stern stuff, and when I walked into the farmyard they were everywhere to be seen. So were the ponies: tall ponies, short ponies, stocky ponies, narrow ponies, what's-going-on? ponies and done-it-all-before ponies.

You could see where a child had plaited a pony itself, and where a kindly adult had lent a hand, and there were little compromises here and there in the manner of dress. No compromises, however, with being warm and waterproof, for country children learn very quickly that he who argues about wearing a coat gets wet.

And so we steamed gently in the half-shelter of the barn, eating hot sausage rolls – proper home-made ones – and telling each other that it might be clearing up. Presently, the Master assigned little groups of children to various adults, and hounds streamed across the farmyard to check out the first patch of cover. This drew blank, but then we were off to the woods, which were bound to hold a fox sheltering from the downpour.

With the land this wet, damage to the fields would heal very quickly, and though the hoofmarks might look dramatic, they would soon disappear. Equally, such going is much easier on horses than when our heavy clay starts to dry out and become holding. When the fox that was in the woods shook off his sleepiness and slipped out of the far end, he proved that the saturated ground was holding scent well.

Truly, this pack of hounds goes from strength to strength, and they are nothing short of magnificent in their work. They hunted their fox with a tremendous cry as little pony legs set off with a will in their wake. Children on foot scrambled heedlessly though the standing water and the drenched turf, doing an amazing job of keeping up.

This most obliging fox gave the youngsters a great gallop as he ran in a wide arc taking in nearly the whole farm, then up to some woodland, where they checked briefly.

We watched him travel along a hedgeline, disappear from sight where he crossed the ditch, reappear where we thought he might, and then he came out of the hedge to cross almost in front of me, where we stood silently so as not to head him away from his chosen route.

Off back to the woods where he had been found, he then, I judged, would lie up and watch our progress.

Behind him, hounds puzzled and sought, using their fox sense where the scent deserted them, trying along the hedgeline, which is where a fox prefers to run. Then a single hound swung his great head and drank in an eddy of scent from the field, swerved towards exactly where the fox had crossed, and another hound, knowing, followed.

Together they owned the scent, pushing across the ride and through the gateway exactly on the fox's line; the huntsman, who had known to leave his hounds alone to do their job, gave us a brief smile and a nod as we told him "They're right!" and cantered past with the body of the pack, the whipper-in bringing the tailhounds.

This was the hunting. Meanwhile, the child-mustering was going just as well, with two good gallops having steadied most of the ponies and settled most of the children. Small groups of less experienced little ones had been marshalled into good viewing points, where they could watch for the fox and perhaps learn a little more of what hounds were doing.

Others were going like smoke in the wake of the hunt staff: over, under, round or through, but determined not to be left behind. From time to time, a breathless parent would arrive and quiz a soaking wet, mud-besmirched child if it wanted to go home yet. I saw no takers!

Roused afresh from the woods, our fox set his mask towards the neighbouring farm, the scent absolutely screaming, the conditions unbelievably wet, and hounds, by the sound of it, very close indeed to their fox.

We had started with more than seventy mounted followers, the greater number of which were children, and the rest adults to whom children had been assigned, not to mention the contingent of children following on foot, and everybody seemed still to be there, still enjoying themselves despite the pouring rain.

Two fields away, hounds ran into their fox: you could tell from their voices. The farmer was there, well pleased. His kindness in allowing us on his land was much appreciated, and we in turn had done a good job by it.

Little groups of followers cantered up, some now ready to take up the offer of "home", more looking as if they could carry on until dusk.
The briefest of respites, and hounds went on to the next draw, keen and businesslike. I had to be home again to see to animals, and so I left them there, working their way across to another farm, another fox, in the pouring rain.

IX

Shimmering like a flock of lapwings, the Brighton and Storrington beagles flickered over the grass, noses glued to the ground. Their sterns were waving like metronomes in a wide arc back and forth as they sifted through the myriad scents of past and present, seeking the one that they were born to follow.

I know plenty of people who have had one pet beagle, but few who chose to repeat the experience, and wisely so. A beagle without a pack is a beagle unfulfilled, no matter how much love it may have from its human friends. The need to hunt, and the need to be part of a pack spells trouble for people who wanted a household pet but find that their little hound is nose down and over the horizon every time it is let off the lead.

This is no fault of either owner or hound, but simply illustrates widely differing requirements. If you see beagles in a pack, working as they have been bred to do since before the Middle Ages, you see beagles radiantly happy, and at their best. Those who have battled with a single beagle would be stunned to see the control that the young huntsman has over his pack. Although every hound is working its very hardest, and concentrating utterly on the job in hand, it takes only a word, a gesture, a note of the horn, to swing the entire pack to where it is needed. It is beautiful to see, and much of the pleasure of beagling is seeing hounds, huntsman and whippers-in working with the fluid harmony that characterises hound work at its very best, a living, shifting kaleidoscope flickering over the fields.

The easy walk of the hunt staff is deceptive: they cross the land in ground-eating strides that barely break rhythm for fence or ditch. The followers too could have you fooled until you take a second look, for many are retired. But their legs are long, and they are as spare and fit as the younger followers, wasting no time, never seeming to hurry, and always well within sight of the action.

However, you do not need to be an athlete to follow the beagles, for if you know your land, or are taken in hand by an experienced beagler, you will soon find the good places to stand and wait for the hunt to come your way.

It is in the nature of the hare to circle, albeit circles measuring some distance, and provided that the pack sticks to the same hare, she will return more or less to the place where she was first roused. Despite some difficult scenting days, and much of the sort of weather that has tested the mettle of the beaglers, this season has been one of the best so far. Socially too the season has been a triumph, for beagling is a very sociable activity, and the pack has travelled up-country to Scotland, Norfolk and Yorkshire, and in return hosted joint meets with the Eton College and Colne Valley.

Attractive as they are, these are working hounds, and it is at their work that they are best seen. One of the followers sees a hare leave her form, and signals with a raised cap, for hounds are a field away. A holloa, and the huntsman effortlessly brings the pack across to hit the line just so. A whimper, a cry, the full-blown chorus of the pack that has lifted human hearts since the dawn of time and has the undiluted power to do so still, and we are off, we are hunting!

X

I set off in the dark, a foul weather forecast preceding me. This was to be my first coursing meet of the season, the previous ones cancelled due to flooding. This season, instead of the ground being too hard from a dry autumn, it was under water. But now the weather deities had given us a nod and a wink, and today was the day.

Hares are not evenly distributed across the country, which leads some misguided folk to think they are rare. Where I live, there is a small hare population that I leave alone unless a landowner invites me to come and course them, an invitation that I am always delighted to receive. Where I was going on this raw dawn was a sporting estate where hares are so plentiful that they are shot at the end of every winter, to keep the numbers down both for the sake of the farmers and the health of the hares themselves. Hares do a terrific amount of damage to crops and forestry, and are also very prone to the effects of overcrowding, suffering stress as well as heavy parasite infestations, both of which kill them slowly and horribly. Before the shooting, greyhounds are invited to come and course, and I go to observe.

The hare fills the eye as the greyhound does: both perfect in symmetry, both designed to the last fibre for the job that they do. Far faster than the greyhound, which is the fastest of dogs, the hare has great cunning, agility and endurance, and will outmatch all but the very best. Run on her own ground, which she knows to the detail, given a start of a hundred yards or more, she gives a dazzling display of athleticism every time she runs, whether chased by a fox, a pet terrier, or an earnest longdog.

The greyhounds, bred in the purple, are built for speed but not endurance, and are without equal for it in the canine world. Their whole demeanour is of quietness and gentleness, yet they are so very keen to do their job. The streamlined muzzles, tiny ears, great eyes, high-knuckled feet, and the immense slant and power in shoulders and quarters exist for that one purpose only. Driven by the awesome engine in that deep chest, powered around the turns by the long tail, they are a miracle of creation. Two by two, they step daintily into slips, one red collar, one white collar, for the judge to know the difference at speed.

The judge's horse dances in the cold wind, though he has a good wool rug over his quarters. The snap of the beaters' flags warns us of their approach, then a cry : "Hare up!"

At once we stand stock-still. Only the hare moves at first, then the slipper, turning his hounds' heads to get them 'sighted', for they are gazehounds and will only chase what they can see. The hare runs dead straight up the field, knowing exactly where she wants to go: sixty yards, seventy, eighty, the slipper starts to lope forward, balancing a hundred and sixty pounds of eager canines. The hare is one hundred and thirty yards in front by the time they stretch out together from the slips, away beautifully even, stride matching stride. They close that distance before you can draw breath.

If you know hares, you know that this one is not in the slightest bit bothered, for both of her ears are raised. Because she can see rearwards as well as to each side and forwards, she knows exactly where her pursuers are, and is getting the measure of them.

As one greyhound drops its head to grasp her, she momentarily drops an ear and turns. The far larger hounds are caught wrongfooted, and she is many lengths away before they recover. She allows them to catch up and repeats the manoeuvre, then drops both ears and a gear to race up the hill, making the hounds accelerate after her before she spins around to run down the hill again, having by far the advantage here with her long back legs and shorter front ones.

The great hounds have almost come to the end of their endurance now, and are lobbing in her wake rather than pressing her. Into the woods she goes, and they pull up, their handlers already running across to catch them. The judge pulls a red or white scarf out of his pocket and holds it in the air to indicate whether red or white collar has won, and canters back to the flag steward, who holds up a flag of the same colour for the benefit of the spectators.

Are hares ever caught? Yes they are: we ran a thirty-two dog stake and caught one hare, which is about average for greyhounds. This hare was caught in a scorching run by a big brindle dog that powered up to her and snatched her off the ground before she realised how fast he was going. The hares are the property of the landowner, and are sold for food. I eat a lot of coursed hares, which rather gives the lie to the fantasy that they are 'torn to pieces' because if they were they could not be sold and nor could I eat them. Much nicer than a shot hare, they don't give the problem of biting on shot, and they are much less messy to prepare. One hare will fed a family twice, and make delicious game soup afterwards.

The rain came on hard just after eleven o'clock, and though I turned my collar and wore my disgraceful but warm tweed hat, I was soon soaked through. I had seen so much fine coursing, so many healthy hares, that I did not mind in the least. Such mastery transcends anything that the sky can throw at us, and I find the elements glorious in their raw power, even when they are at their most uncomfortable. My coat took four days to dry, but the memories of that wonderful day will be with me for ever.

XI

Drenched in yellow-clay wealden mud, relaxed and happy, led by the merry pack and the huntsman blowing 'home' the hunt followers came up the lane from the stubble fields and into the farm drive where we had all been invited to a traditional hunting tea. The footfollowers would be in first, with only themselves to organise, or perhaps an accompanying dog to towel dry and leave snug in a blanket. The hunt staff would be in last, for tired wet horses must first be taken back to their stables, and wearier, wetter hounds returned to their lodge, where each would be checked over individually. Mounted followers would see their horses set fair, some with help, some doing everything themselves, before they saw to their own comfort. This all meant that we fitted into the farmhouse in natural relays.

With carpets and chairs protected by plastic and dustsheets, neat rows of soaking boots and running shoes left on the step, besmotered footfollowers relaxed in the warmth and hospitality that was such a welcome contrast to the raw cold and wet outside. Some had even unsocked, the reason being that their socks were every bit as filthy as their boots. Vast lengths of naked foot and leg were thus visible, but fortunately the ladies were made of stern stuff, and none fainted.

Trays of scrambled free-range eggs were demolished, along with crispy bacon and mushrooms, piles of fragrant toast, endless good tea, coffee or orange juice, good conversation, good humour.

In came the mounted followers, bootless, hatless, soaking coats removed and replaced with warm sweaters or fleeces, faces ruddy from the fresh air, each of us filling in the gaps of the day's events: did you see what happened here, were you able to follow there?

Vacate the table for the newcomers, stand with your back to the fire and munch fruit cake or iced cake, all home-made. Just a touch of port? No thank you, I'm driving, but this tea is so good, and I'll have another cup with pleasure.

Meanwhile the children have found the hound puppies, or the hound puppies have found the children, giggles and thundering coming from the drawing room, where strictly speaking, neither should be. One couple of beagles, one of foxhounds; they may be 'pups' but the latter are huge and so are the pawmarks. Our hosts have seen it all before, and remain good-humoured. On the back step sits a foxhound pup between three children, his eyes slits of pleasure and the biggest beam on his face as he is stroked and cuddle within an inch of his life, and secrets are whispered into his long tan ears.

His brother is at present demonstrating his superb nose by tracking down the plate of cakes and its attendant giggle of children. There is no mistaking the fact that his comprehension of the word 'No' involves a time limit beyond which it could not possibly apply, at least to him.

More people arrive: more chairs are vacated, more backs move to the fire as the early arrivals prepare to depart, but hunting talk is in full flow, and we linger.

I am taken to see a splendid young terrier, already showing her working instincts, and three graceful longdogs tread softly among the visitors. They are too dignified to beg, you understand, but if you did happen to find that piece of cake too much for you, it is indicated that it would be well received.

Outside, the rain seems even colder now that darkness has set in. At last the hunt staff return, a fresh platter of hot food ready just right to welcome them. What a splendid tradition, what wonderful hospitality.

Though there is still much work at home for most of us, we set out into the winter evening glowing, the events of the day fresh and uplifting in our hearts. I can picture today's children as adults, warming their backs at a big log fire, talking over the events of the day, with their own children hugging a hound on the kitchen steps. Long may it all continue.

XII

I am at the point of the wood where it will leave, whatever 'it' is. Accompanied by a terrier and a lurcher, I have the beater's job. I have entered the wood at the low end, and am gently working the cover around in an arc, up to the high part where game wants to go, and then artfully, subtly down to the thickest stands of fallen trees, brambles and deep wet ground, where anything could lie up, and take a deal of shifting if it has.

When the stick can be spared from its duties of keeping me upright, I tap it against a tree; now and then, when my breathing allows, I utter the sharp, purring traditional cry of the beater. The ground is boot-losingly sticky, and wet rank herbage dangles from the trees.

Below and to one side, just right to keep watch, is the man with the gun.

Shaded by sweeping branches, thigh-deep in thicket, he is at once relaxed and alert. There is all sorts in this wood, and any of it could come out at any time. Sometimes there is nothing in here that we would wish to shoot, and sometimes there is more than enough.

I don't use my voice much except to indicate a critical change of route, for I want to move the quarry through slowly. The dogs, with no such inhibitions and only the most basic grasp of logistics, barrel through at their own pace, a sudden crackling rush from the otherwise silent lurcher or a series of yaps from the terrier indicating that game is afoot.

I have been on the business end of the wood on many occasions as well. I know the tearing-calico screech of the jay, the harsh rattle of the magpie, the 'gaaah!' of the crow, tracking the movement of beater, dogs or vermin. I know the soft whiffling of grasses at the very edge of the covert that heralds a sharp, pointed mask and the rapid departure of a fox, quite distinct from the rhythmic accelerating crashing of undergrowth out of which a roe will erupt. I know the clattering rattle of a pheasant taking off, or the silent, jinking flight of a woodcock.

A stoat is just suddenly there. In the woods, a flock of birds could get up and wheel around the beater; by the standing gun a wren may perch, impossibly delicate and quite unafraid. Ploughing steadily through the unforgiving ground, the beater has to judge when to make a noise, when to keep quiet, when to bring the dogs in, or cheer them on.

The dogs trust me utterly. I never lie to them, and they know if I send them on that there will be something there. Only fools lie to dogs. We have a series of signals, honed through years of hunting together, so that they and the standing gun know what is ahead of them. I, with human height and human colour vision am better placed to see the low russet flicker that is a fox, the hodden-grey flurry and flashing white of a rabbit, the bulky dun of a winter deer. They, with their incredible sense of smell, translate foot-scent and air-scent with computer precision into species, gender, condition and distance ahead. I know when to guide them and when to leave them; they know when to heed me and when to forgive me.

I cross the second loop of the stream, testing the going carefully with my stick before committing a leg to it, and then up to where my colleague is, and the two wagging dogs.

We have not moved much game today, but no matter; if it isn't there it can't come out, and everywhere about is rather wet. There are places up the hill which will be more lively, I have no doubt.

"There was a woodcock" he tells me, "But it wasn't a safe shot."
We are both happy for that.

Over the single strand of ancient barbed wire and along the run of the boundary stream, then with the dogs questing ahead, and that feeling not just of happiness but of everything being exactly right, and you becoming a part of it, that you get with roughshooting, or any other fieldsport come to that.

The low winter sun gilds the hedgerows, and all is well.

XIII

Animals that hunt by scent know the importance of scenting conditions. Last night's heavy rain sowed the seed for today's superb scenting, and what better way to celebrate than with a pack of hounds?

Here in these ancient woods, where hunting and shooting interests maintain a conservationist's dream, the foxes normally lie tight in the dead bracken and living rhododendron, knowing that the scent of each will mask their own. But this morning the warm scent of fox will overlay the wet vegetation, and, knowing this, a fox is away sharpish, two hundred yards from the first hound entering the thicket.

The deep roaring bay of a single hound is overtaken like running water with the melodious voices of his companions; for an instant, the whole glorious tableau freeze-frames before us. Hounds in, fox out, horses wheeling, horn doubling, then we are off, pounding hooves throwing mud into the air, the creak of leather and jingle of lorinery, breath rising opaque over steaming horses, and a well-known voice on the parallel ride to tell us where our quarry has crossed.

The hunger of the empty months without hunting* is only just beginning to ease, though we have been out since just before Christmas. Diverse miracles have been performed to bring us together now, and few can guess at the trials and traumas involved in bringing a pack of hounds to this standard under these conditions. Not only do hounds look a picture, they are hunting up a storm, all beauty, power and intent. There is a great backlog to make up, where the fox controllers could not get onto the land to do their job at the proper time, which means there is a large concentration of foxes in areas that cannot support them. A local farmer in the midst of lambing has seen nine foxes on the land in the space of two hours, three of them in a group harrying the in-lamb ewes in a single field. By these attacks, ewes can be terrorised into giving birth too early, the lambs lost, the ewes bereft and often in need of veterinary treatment. Healthy full-term lambs are commonly taken as well, for though lambing itself is conducted indoors, lambs need fresh air and exercise in order to grow, and must go out as soon as possible. A pair of foxes working a field of ewes and lambs will set the young ones panicking and running blindly, until one of a pair is far enough away from its mother for a fox to grab and kill. The importance of the role of hunting in splitting up groups of foxes and keeping them moving as well as thinning them out is often underestimated. We are certainly seeing the results of not being able to do this in due time, though the hound work has been incredible since our late start, and much ground has already been caught up.

Equally vital is the role of the terriers, which are hard at work almost every day. Indeed, they have just been summoned, and the quad-bike is on its way with the dedicated young men and their varminty tykes. Huntsman and hounds go forth to draw again in the meantime, knowing that the job is in good hands.

In with the pack, out with the fox from a long tongue of dense woodland. The vanguard of half a dozen experienced hounds follows exactly on its trail, and then comes a small group of younger ones, strong legs but half-trained noses, trying hard but not quite there yet.
Shouldering through them comes an old hound, dark-coloured, nose glued to the precise line that the fox has taken, belling voice proclaiming his truth. Falling-in like the junior recruits that they are, the youngsters tuck in behind him, the rest of the pack surging through, our huntsman on a converging track at a squelching gallop. Pure magic.

*This is the year 2002, when foot-and-mouth disrupted the countryside and delayed the start of the hunting season.

The horses think so too. There is the trace-clipped bay pony being kept fit by Mother until school holidays, the tall elegant black horse well into his teens carrying the petite lady, over here a hot-headed youngster overcome by excitement and giving his rider something to concentrate upon, then the trio of five-next-birthdays with their eyes standing out like chapel hat-pegs, while the old-enough-to-know-betters dance and foam and roll their eyes.

There is a little group of point-to-pointers, all slender legs and doe eyes, and a big bay hunter that fills the eye with his good looks and quality. You can tell by his demeanour that he is good rather than quiet; as we are woodland hunting, he seems to say, he will go when he is asked and wait when it is necessary but ah! he is capable of so much more. No doubt back at the stable he keeps the T-shirt that says he has been there and done that.

I have work to do at home and so must leave, but the air has changed, waiting for nightfall, and I doubt that the hunt will stay out for much longer. A woodcock flickers across the path in front of me as I make my way back, and the feeling is of utter contentment: hounds in a winter landscape and all's right with the world.

XIV

A scruffy little, grey little, flimsy little dog, 'a rag, a bone and a hank of hair' in Kipling's words, a dog that looks as if a puff of wind would blow him over, a dog that views the world through bright amber eyes as old as Time. His shape has something of the whippet about it, overlaid with a cobweb of slate blue hair, but his strong jaw and those deep, knowing eyes come from the bedlington terrier. He has great charm about him, but he is all hound.

Small dogs are often underrated, but it must not be forgotten that, until a very few decades ago, no dog was kept that did not have a purpose. Big dogs guarded, medium dogs kept the flocks and herds, all dogs hunted. Even ladies' lapdogs had a purpose beyond entertaining their owners, several purposes in fact: they attracted parasites that would otherwise feast on people, they provided warmth in cold, draughty rooms, but most of all, they killed small vermin, rats and mice, that scurried about in houses great and small.

Now we have whole generations of people who cannot realise how pernicious the rodent problem used to be in days gone past, when every night-time heralded the pattering and gnawing, when rats and mice scampered over people a-bed, and bit the babies in their cradles, ran amok in larders and cupboards ruining stored food, and shredded rugs and draperies.

Little dogs can be fearless ratters and mousers, much more efficient than any cat. Most cat owners I know complain that puss brings live rodents into the house and then lets them go. But the small dogs kill with a snap and a flick, just as they have for centuries, whether spoiled lapdogs or not.

The little fellow with me today hunts on ahead, testing every tussock for scent. Anything is grist to his mill: mouse, rat, squirrel, stoat, mink, and of course rabbit. He will flush pheasant, partridge, snipe and woodcock for the gun, yes, and retrieve them too, and his owner has a high regard for him. So have I.

He bundles fearlessly into an overgrown ditch, his progress marked by crackling and the odd splash, his wise little head peering out at intervals to check where I am. There are not many rabbits about at present, following probably the most virulent strain of myxomatosis that we have had for some years, but here is one, leaving the reeds almost at my feet. In fact, I touch its fleeing body as it passes, but rabbits are slippery things and it runs straight through my fingers.

There follows a grand hunt in and out of the sedges, the brambles, the hawthorn, blackthorn and briar, up and down the ditch, the little dog working like a hero, using his nose all the time. I parallel his progress on the path, watching him lose the scent and then casting about to find it again, watching him bolt the rabbit and lose it once more. At one point, the rabbit sits right beside me, having failed to notice my presence at all. Its white scut, its rump and hindquarters are clearly visible, its forehand hidden in long grass. I could pick it up, but a sense of fair play stays my hand. With so few rabbits about at the moment it is hardly the pest that it would have been before harvest; let the little dog work, and if he catches it or misses it, that is the way of the natural world.

The rabbit realises its error all of a sudden and leaps away from me. There is a crash and a great splash that indicates the whole dog is now in the ditch. Bunny scoots up the bank, across the track and into a rabbit hole, the dog missing by a heartbeat. He looks down the rabbit hole, his entire body in a frown, then regards me long and hard. We'll give that one best, lad: it was a good contest.

He is too experienced a dog to paw ineffectively at rabbit holes, so after one last burning glance he returns to my heels.

Much of the footpath is flooded, and there are sheets of standing water in the fields. Wading birds are making use of this in the gathering dusk. The sky we walk under is magenta and dove grey, and bird-talk is all around us. But our homeward path lies eastwards, our back to the setting sun, and so is much darker once we turn onto it.

Thus it was that he saw the hare and I did not. He hurdled the brook with a mighty leap that had him airborne for what seemed like a couple of seconds, and then touched down running across the heavy tilth. The hare, which had been in the act of rising from her form, began to test her pursuer.

First she ran straight to assess his speed. She has almost all-round vision but for a small blind spot behind and in front of her, and therefore wanted to keep him in sight. So she settled to a speed that allowed him close but no closer, while she tried his mettle. Ah, a fast dog then.

She let him closer, then spun around: he matched her, his small size allowing him little ground lost but not the length of stride that a larger dog would have. Agile, then – have to be careful of this one.

Then she feinted to one side and leapt to the other, catching him out completely, thus learning that he had no experience of running hares, which is true enough, being neither bred nor wanted for that job. Again, his stride meant that he had to work hard to make up lost ground, as well as the fact that he was sinking into the heavy wet clay that the hare was skimming over. She allowed him as far as her desired distance and then proceeded to play with him, running, turning, feinting, taking him all over the field, completely in charge of the situation and quite unworried.

You could video this display of mastery, add loud music, maybe some thrilling drumbeats and an emotional commentary and make it seem as if the hare was in terrible distress, panicking and in danger of her very life – but only if you showed it to people who knew nothing of hares. Those experienced in the matter of coursing would know that a hare running with her ears up is well within herself, that a hare dropping an ear as she turns is simply calculating her manoeuvre to a hair's breadth, and they would see at once that the hare is turning the dog, not the dog turning the hare.

She could leave the dog standing at any time she chose, but instead was testing him, much in the way a crow will flap a few yards from a dog and land again, goading it to chase.

She ran the little hound for maybe a minute and a half before bringing him back to me in a wide arc, leaving him with a flourish and probably a comment on the lines of "See you again, same time, same place" as she accelerated into the dusk.

He, having lost sight of her, bounded back over the brook and cantered up to me. Though he had certainly done some work, his breathing quickly returned to normal, showing how fit he was. Despite having lost his quarry, he was very pleased with himself, and almost at once put his nose down and started hunting again. He put up another rabbit not far from where I had left the vehicle, pursuing it with undiminished eagerness, finally nailing it on the edge of the muckheap. Sadly, the rabbit was myxomatosed, so I left it for the scavengers of the night rather than bearing it home in triumph for his supper.

My brief had been to 'take him and tire him out, please,' from an owner who was temporarily laid up, and while I had not fulfilled that task quite to the letter, I felt sure that the little fellow would sleep well tonight.

Jem was striding up the sidehill like a young'un when I found him in the beating line. He's been beating since he was a scrawny nipper in his brother's hand-me-downs, and though the last few seasons it looked as if the years had finally caught up with him, and he had more time on 'stop' duty than actual beating, he was pulling up the slope with barely a hint of breathlessness today.

It was Jem who taught me a lot of what I know today: he looked after my first ferret when I was not allowed to have any at home, and it was Jem who found me my first lurcher pup and showed me how to train her. One of his fingers was broken and crooked from a trapping accident, and he would impress upon me always to spring a trap with a stick before I moved it. Many's the time I was impatient and thought not to bother, and then those words and the image of Jem's hand would swim before my eyes, and I'd go and find a stick.

The drives we beat all had names. Sometimes the origins were forgotten in time, sometimes Jem would be the only person to recollect why there was a Friar's Bottom nowhere near a monastery, or an Apricot Grove in which no apricot had ever been seen to grow. I talked Jem through where we would go for the day, drive by drive, after discussing the weather and the way the birds should fly. He was always quick to point out little bits of the wild world that others might not notice, and so instilled in me the habit of seeing rather than just looking. Though his bright grey-blue eyes were clear today, there had been a time when they did not see as well as when he was young, so I would tell him how the cover-crop was looking after the gales, how the trees were unleafing following the frost, and whether the geese had come into the wildbrooks. We had old jokes and shared memories, such as when someone had shot a goose the other side of the rife, and his terrier had leaped across, started to retrieve it and then sat on the far bank and eaten it before his eyes. He remembered the fallow buck that took on the landrover one autumn, and the incredible course one of my dogs had on the black fox. Jem took me out when I was nothing but a nuisance youngster, and had the patience to show me his world. I have been in thrall to Nature ever since.

The south downs have a way about them: you think you have got to the top and then another slope billows before you. There was time to stop and catch our breath, look around at the fields, the stubbles and plough, what was down to winter crops, where the sheep were folded, up from the East Sussex marshes. We heard the 'peeeyooo' of an overflying buzzard, while away to the quarries, a kestrel hovered. Pity I hadn't brought my young dog today, he said, for there was a hare, look, just right. The going was too flinty, we agreed, so maybe it was just as well, but you couldn't beat the sight of a good dog at the back of a good hare.

Still he was full of energy, eager to get to the top, so we started up again, the clouds gathering steel and pewter with the promise of weather ahead. We paused again at the brow, and delighted in the sight of a pack

of beagles spread out casting for scent on the plough far below. What a treat to see. Jem had been a keen beagler up until a few years ago.

This was our last drive now. Having topped the hill, we slid and stepped awkwardly downwards, through the thickets and along the chalk, the

old-man's-beard, the briar and bramble snatching at our clothes or winding cunningly about our feet. The smooth trunk of the fallen beech beckoned us on, pale in the half-light of day fading into greenleaf shadow. The guns were laughing and joking at the foot of the valley, tired dogs scratching and wagging at their heels as they sleeved their shotguns and made ready for the homeward journey. Weary beaters and pickers-up said their goodbyes and see-you-next-times. The gamekeeper beckoned Jem and me over, with a "don't forget to take an extra brace" as he handed us our pheasants.

"What did you bring those filthy things here for?" Jem's daughter, Eileen, furious face, never had liked me for the time I spent with her father. I had come straight from the shoot to see him, not stopping to change or tidy up. I nodded in the direction of the old man to show her why. There he was, sitting up against the pillows and far, far away, his gnarled, crippled old hands deep in the feathers of a brace of pheasants, and a radiant smile on his lifeless face.

FINIS